HORRIBLE SCIENCE

FRIGHTENING ~LIGHT~

Nick Arnold

Illustrated by
Tony De Saulles

SCHOLASTIC INC.

New York   Toronto   London   Auckland   Sydney
Mexico City   New Delhi   Hong Kong   Buenos Aires

ISBN 0-439-20724-X

Text copyright © 1999 by Nick Arnold.
Illustrations copyright © 1999 by Tony De Saulles.

All rights reserved. Published by Scholastic Inc., 555 Broadway, New York, NY
10012, by arrangement with Scholastic Children's Books, a division of Scholastic
Ltd. SCHOLASTIC and associated logos are trademarks and/or registered
trademarks of Scholastic Inc.

12 11 10 9 8 7 6 5 4 3 2 1   0 1 2 3 4 5 6/0

Printed in the U.S.A.   40
First Scholastic printing, February 2002

Contents

Nick Arnold has been writing stories and books since he was young, but never dreamed he'd find fame writing about frightening light. His research involved tripping up in the dark, staring down the wrong end of telescopes, and trying on glasses, and he enjoyed every minute of it.

When he's not delving into Horrible Science, he spends his spare time teaching adults in a college. His hobbies include eating pizza, riding his bike, and thinking up corny jokes (though not all at the same time).

Tony De Saulles picked up his crayons when he was still in diapers and has been doodling ever since. He takes Horrible Science very seriously and even agreed to draw an eclipse as it happened. Unfortunately, he couldn't find his crayons in the dark.

When he's not out with his sketchpad, Tony likes to write poetry and play squash, though he hasn't written any poetry about squash yet.

INTR🔆DUCTION

Science is frightening. Frighteningly confusing.

Take the topic of light. You see light every day in sunshine and light bulbs so you might think that the science of light would be light work.

But you'd be wrong. It's hard. Harder to crack than a dried pea from last semester's school lunch. And as for the facts — they're harder to untangle than a vat of spaghetti.

See what I mean? Light = instant confusion! It's frightening. And if you ask a scientist to explain about light, it's even worse. You're bound to get a long, incomprehensible answer with lots of frighteningly complicated scientific words.

Horrible, isn't it? Yep — it's not surprising that science can make your flesh creep.

Well, now to look on the bright side — here's a little light relief for you. Simply take this book to a quiet place, sit down and turn the pages. It will shed light on light science, and there are lots of light-hearted facts about eyeballs and laser surgery and ghostly lights and other dark and horrible corners of science. These could really brighten your day — especially when you frighten your teacher with a few tricky questions.

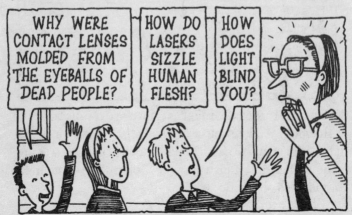

Your new-found knowledge of light science is sure to put your teacher in the shade. And afterward, who knows? You might even become a leading light in science — then you'll really enjoy the limelight! So now there's only one question.

Are you bright enough to read on?

SEEING THE LIGHT

The sun was sinking behind the Brocken Mountain. The sky was getting darker by the minute and already the climber could scarcely see the narrow twisting goat-path at his feet. The climber was beginning to feel very afraid.

"It's time," he thought. "I'm going to see it any minute," and he looked anxiously at his pocket watch.

"Pull yourself together!" he said to himself. "You're a scientist. There must be a rational explanation. There's no such thing as ghosts."

But he trembled and his mouth felt dry as he wondered for the first time how he would find his way down in the dark. A bead of cold sweat trickled down his neck.

Suddenly his heart started thudding. Tiny hairs prickled on the back of his neck.

Somehow he knew even without a backward glance that he was not alone. There was someone . . . or something on the mountain behind him. He tried to turn his head but his neck had locked rigid. At last he forced his whole body to swing round. His jaw dropped open in horror. Behind him, etched on the dimming clouds was a huge dark figure. Light played around its ghostly outline as it hung in the air.

The thing seemed to be watching him. Waiting. Waiting to pounce.

For a moment the climber seemed hypnotized. Then he forced himself to react. With trembling hands he pulled out a pocket book and a chewed stub of pencil. And started scribbling unreadable notes. All the time he was mumbling desperately.

"Fascinating phenomenon," he said, over and over again. "Fascinating. I — uh — better get moving."

As the climber turned and scurried up the path the giant figure seemed to spring into life. It began climbing silently and effortlessly in the climber's footsteps. And whatever it was, it was coming after him, silently — faster and faster.

And reaching out its long shadowy arms . . .

DON'T PANIC! As the scientist realized, the figure was only his own shadow. This very real if ghostly effect is called the specter of the Brocken after the Brocken Mountain in Germany where it's often seen. If you climb a mountain near sunset (not a very safe thing to do — so don't try it on your own) the low sun can cast your shadow on nearby clouds. And you see a huge ghostly figure. But this is just one of many horribly amazing light effects.

Read on for the frightening facts.

Frightening light fact file

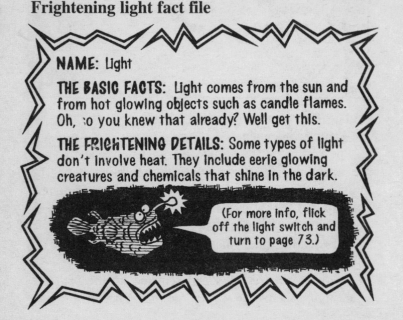

NAME: Light

THE BASIC FACTS: Light comes from the sun and from hot glowing objects such as candle flames. Oh, so you knew that already? Well get this.

THE FRIGHTENING DETAILS: Some types of light don't involve heat. They include eerie glowing creatures and chemicals that shine in the dark.

(For more info, flick off the light switch and turn to page 73.)

A gloomy thought

So you really did switch out the lights just then? Well, put them back on and read this.

It's easy to make light appear and disappear, isn't it? Every morning light appears in the sky and you don't even have to get out of bed to make it happen. So maybe that's why people take light for granted. And think it's no big deal.

Well, it is.

Imagine the sun doesn't rise tomorrow. Then imagine that all the light bulbs in the world go *phfutt* at the same instant.

And imagine also that even the distant stars fail to shine. The world would be very cold and very dark. And frightening and dangerous. Without light to see by, people would be bumping into each other and treading on the cat and knocking over priceless ornaments and skidding on banana skins.

And that's not all. Can you figure out which other things you need light for?

Frightening light quiz

Without sunlight you can't see:
1. A rainbow. TRUE/FALSE
2. The moon. TRUE/FALSE

If it's completely dark:
3. Your face wouldn't appear in a mirror. TRUE/FALSE

4. You couldn't take vacation pictures. TRUE/FALSE
5. A poisonous rattlesnake couldn't find where you are hiding. TRUE/FALSE

1. TRUE. A rainbow happens when sunlight shines through droplets of rain. This splits the sunlight into different colors. (Check out pages 28-32 for the colorful details.) You actually get rainbows at night made by moonlight but the colors are too dim for your eyes to make out.

2. TRUE. The moon doesn't make its own light. That pretty silvery moonlight is actually sunlight that's bounced off (or as a scientist might say, reflected from) the moon. The surface of the moon is made of rock and dust, but if it was ice, it would reflect light really well and the moon would be nearly as bright as the sun.

3. TRUE. A mirror works by reflecting light. There's nothing to keep you from looking at the bathroom mirror in the dark. But since there's no light, the mirror won't reflect your image. Keep in mind, according to legend, if you're a vampire the mirror won't show your image anyway.

4. TRUE. Imagine you went exploring in a dark cave and left your flashlight at home. Whoops. You couldn't take any pictures because the chemicals that make a photograph only work if light falls on the film. **5. FALSE.** The rattlesnake has a pit on each side of its head full of temperature sensors. These detect heat from your body. It's frightening. And that's why hiding from the snake in a dark closet isn't such a clever idea.

13

The light fantastic

So light brightens up our lives. But take a closer look at light and it's even more fantastic. Imagine you could look at a ray of light through an incredibly powerful microscope. It would have to be billions of times more powerful than the world's most powerful microscope. Here's what you might see.

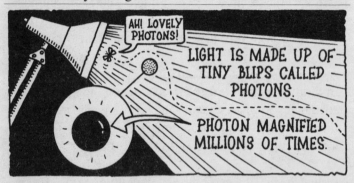

Photons are never still — they zig-zag tens of billions of times a second to form light waves. And hundreds of light waves could stretch across this period.

Sounds a bit strange, doesn't it? Well, just imagine a wave at the beach made by a single drop of water that whizzes around so fast it seems to be everywhere at once.

A note to the reader

At this point we were going to ask a scientist to give us a long, boring account of photons. But you wouldn't read it, would you? So here's a thrilling cartoon strip with the same info. Oh dear, it looks as if the scientist has something to say after all.

A QUICK SCIENTIFIC NOTE

Sorry to break in. Before you get into the cartoon you need to know the following fact: an atom is a tiny ball of matter. It's so small that one million atoms could stretch across the thickness of this page. Every chemical in the universe is made of different atoms or mixtures of atoms. OK, got all that?

THE ADVENTURES OF SUPER-PHOTON

IS IT A BIRD? IS IT A PLANE? NO. IT'S SUPER-PHOTON!

The story so far...

HI!

Super-Photon was born deep inside the sun. He leaped fully formed from a super-heated atom.

ZERO! Super-Photon weighs nothing at all. He's much too small to see, much smaller even than an atom.

But he has awesome superhuman energy drawn from electric and magnetic forces in the sun. He zig-zags to and fro 600,000,000,000,000 times a second to form a light wave. And he never runs out of energy

Continued...

17

Bet you never knew!

1. Actually, there's nothing special about Super-Photon. The sun produces trillions of photons every second and there's nothing remarkable about Super-Photon's powers.

2. Every day thousands of billions of these tiny blips of energy travel 93,210,000 miles (150,000,000 km) through the wastes of space just to whack you! But because photons don't weigh anything you don't feel them smacking into your head.

3. You might wonder what happens to photons after they hit something. Well, remember a photon is just a blip of energy. It hits an atom and its energy is soaked up. So it's bye-bye photon. But photons do much more than whiz around.

Dare you discover . . . what light can do?

To begin with:

Wrap some aluminum foil around the end of a small bright flashlight.

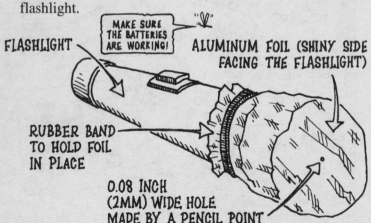

FLASHLIGHT

MAKE SURE THE BATTERIES ARE WORKING!

ALUMINUM FOIL (SHINY SIDE FACING THE FLASHLIGHT)

RUBBER BAND TO HOLD FOIL IN PLACE

0.08 INCH (2MM) WIDE HOLE MADE BY A PENCIL POINT

What you need:

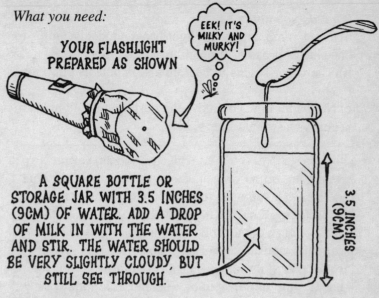

YOUR FLASHLIGHT
PREPARED AS SHOWN

EEK! IT'S MILKY AND MURKY!

A SQUARE BOTTLE OR STORAGE JAR WITH 3.5 INCHES (9CM) OF WATER. ADD A DROP OF MILK IN WITH THE WATER AND STIR. THE WATER SHOULD BE VERY SLIGHTLY CLOUDY, BUT STILL SEE THROUGH.

3.5 INCHES (9CM)

Experiment 1:
1. Place the jar in front of a dark object. A dark book or some gloomy wallpaper will do.
2. Put your flashlight up to the sides of the jar and switch on the light. You should be able to see the beam of light.
3. Now shine the light up so it hits the underside of the water.

What do you notice?
a) The light seems to flicker like a broken TV.
b) The light dances sideways.
c) The light seems to bounce down at an angle.

Experiment 2:
Now place the flashlight about 2 inches (5 cm) away from the sides of the jar. Try shining the light up or down from different angles.

19

What do you notice?

a) From some angles the light beam suddenly jumps to one side as it passes through the sides of the jar.

b) The water begins to heat up and bubble as you move the light.

c) No matter how you move the flashlight the light beam is always a straight line.

Answers:

1. c) The light bounces (reflects) off the underside of the water. The surface of the water is very smooth and the photons of light can all reflect in the same direction.

2. a) Light doesn't always go in a straight line. When light travels from air to water it slows 140,000 miles (224,900 km) per second. This is because the photons have to push through lots of atoms in the water — just imagine a crowd of people trying to run through another crowd. When a beam of light hits the water at an angle one side of the beam slows before the other. This makes the beam bend.

Frightening expressions

One astronomer says to another:

Is this ref action something to do with a football match?

Answer:
No. Scientists call the bending of light refraction.

By now you'll have realized:
1. There's more to light than meets the eye.
2. That light is horribly amazing.
But you might also feel puzzled. If photons are so tiny and so fast how come scientists know so much about them? I mean, you can't exactly catch photons in a butterfly net. Well, it took the combined brain power of some frighteningly bright scientists to discover the truth.

TURN THE PAGE
AND DISCOVER HOW
THEY DID IT. . .

Much of our knowledge of light is based on the work of two scientific geniuses, Isaac Newton (1642-1727) and Albert Einstein (1879-1955). However, lots of scientists lent a hand. Well, as they say "many hands make LIGHT work," ha ha. Here's a handy guide to scientists who study light.

Spot the scientist

1. Physicists

INTERESTED IN: physical forces that shape the world - stuff like heat or electricity. The actual type of physicist featured in this book is an optical physicist. And - you guessed it - they study light.

WHAT THEY DO: set up experiments, make calculations about the speed of light and other exciting topics.

WHERE THEY WORK: university laboratories.

NOTE: physicists can be rather scruffy and absent-minded about their clothes. This is because they're too busy thinking about complex experiments to worry about how they look.

THOUGHTS ABOUT COMPLEX EXPERIMENTS

2. Astronomers

INTERESTED IN: stars and planets and other things you find in outer space. Astronomers are interested in light because we can only see space objects because of the light they produce or reflect.

WHAT THEY DO: scan the night sky using telescopes.

WHERE THEY WORK: observatories.

NOTE: astronomers are very hard to spot. They're shy, nocturnal (night-living) creatures who emerge after dark to study the night sky.

CLOSE-UP OF RARE PHOTO SHOWING ASTRONOMER CREEPING OUT TO HER OBSERVATORY AT NIGHT

3. Ophthalmologists

INTERESTED IN: eyeballs, their diseases, and how they work.

WHAT THEY DO: they're trained doctors who treat patients with eye problems. Some are surgeons who perform operations on the eye.

WHERE THEY WORK: hospital eye departments.

NOTE: it's hard to find an ophthalmologist because they're always busy. Lots of people have sight problems, you see?

Pulling a fast one

For centuries scientists were determined to measure the speed of light. They knew that this would help them judge the distance of planets and so make more accurate astronomical observations. So lots of scientists took a shot. But they had a problem. Light is kind of speedy. All light photons zoom along at 186,282 miles (299,792,458 meters) a second. There's nothing faster in the known universe — not even kids leaving a science class on a Friday afternoon.

Now, you'd think it would be impossible to measure the speed of light. I mean, you'd need amazingly quick reactions and a very good stopwatch to do it — right? So how did scientists manage this impossible feat? First to try was Italian scientist Galileo Galilei (1564-1642).

Gallant Galileo

One dark night Galileo and a friend went into the mountains. Each man carried a lantern with a shutter.

Galileo climbed a hill. His friend climbed another hill three kilometers away. It was a cold, lonely and dangerous trek and if either man had fallen there was no hope of a quick rescue.

Once he reached the top of his hill Galileo opened the shutter of his lantern and started counting. The plan was for the friend to show his lantern in response to Galileo's signal.

To his relief Galileo saw the light from his friend's lantern and stopped counting.

Could you be a scientist?

But the great scientist was wrong. In fact, Galileo found this out for himself when he and his long-suffering friend climbed hills further apart but found that the light signal still seemed to take the same time. Why was this?

Answer:
Light is so fast that the difference of a few kilometers makes almost no difference to the time it takes to complete its journey. In fact, Galileo and his pal were simply timing how quickly they reacted to the light signals. Galileo figured this out and gave up.

Light speed clocked

Using complex calculations astronomers were also trying to measure the speed of light and one of them, British astronomer James Bradley (1693-1762) came up with a figure in 1725. He used data such as the angle of his telescope and the speed of the Earth as it whizzes round the sun. He was only five per cent off!

Meanwhile, back in the hills. In 1849 French physicist Armand Fizeau (1819-1896) shone a bright light from the top of a hill. The light shone through the spokes of a spinning wheel and bounced off a mirror on a hilltop five miles (eight km) distant before returning through the wheel.

I WORKED OUT THE SPEED OF LIGHT BY MEASURING THE DISTANCE THE WHEEL TRAVELLED, ITS SPEED AND THE DISTANCE LIGHT TRAVELLED

THAT'S 'WHEELY' CLEVER!

His figure of 194,700 miles (313,300 km) per second was a bit too speedy. But the technique proved to be a bright idea and was used by other scientists.

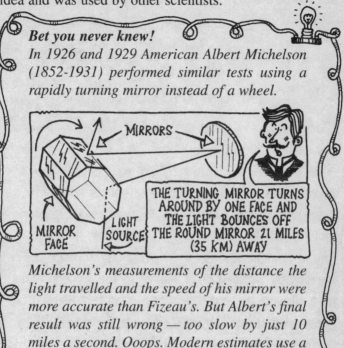
Izzy the incredible

One scientist played a key role in bringing the secrets of light to light — he was Isaac Newton. Of course, any old teacher will tell you that Newton is famous for describing the forces that can affect a moving object — forces such as gravity. But do they also know that Newton's pet dog was named Diamond? Now Diamond wasn't quite as smart as his brainy owner. Here's what his diary might have looked like if he'd learned to write.

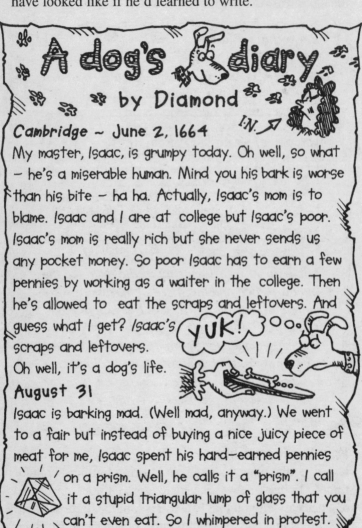

A dog's diary
by Diamond

Cambridge ~ June 2, 1664

My master, Isaac, is grumpy today. Oh well, so what — he's a miserable human. Mind you his bark is worse than his bite — ha ha. Actually, Isaac's mom is to blame. Isaac and I are at college but Isaac's poor. Isaac's mom is really rich but she never sends us any pocket money. So poor Isaac has to earn a few pennies by working as a waiter in the college. Then he's allowed to eat the scraps and leftovers. And guess what I get? Isaac's scraps and leftovers.

YUK!

Oh well, it's a dog's life.

August 31

Isaac is barking mad. (Well mad, anyway.) We went to a fair but instead of buying a nice juicy piece of meat for me, Isaac spent his hard-earned pennies on a prism. Well, he calls it a "prism". I call it a stupid triangular lump of glass that you can't even eat. So I whimpered in protest.

Isaac looked down at me in surprise.

"Are you OK?" he asked.

My master often talks to me because he doesn't have too many human friends.

"I'm rough," I replied.

Actually it sounded more like "ruff!" so Isaac ignored me. Well, he's still working and I'm dog-tired. So I'm taking my grumbling belly off to bed.

Woolsthorpe, Lincolnshire ~ December 25, 1665

We're here staying with Isaac's mom. It's all because of something called "the plague". Well, humans are dropping dead like flies and the college is closed. So we came here. It's a good thing this plague. Now I get fed regularly by Isaac's mom. Yum, yum — Christmas goose bones.

January 1, 1666

My master missed supper ... again. As usual, he's up in his room scribbling masses of meaningless numbers and mumbling scientific gibberish about light. He never washes or changes his clothes — phwoar, he's really going to the dogs. Mind you, I'm always ready to help my master. That's why I made sure I was around to eat his supper for him. At least it didn't go to waste!

January 12

I sneaked into Isaac's room today. Got a bit of a shock. Isaac has made a small hole in the shutters. (I bet his mom will have a fit when she sees the damage.) A ray of light shone through the hole and made a blob of sunlight on the wall. This proves my theory — Isaac *is* completely bonkers.

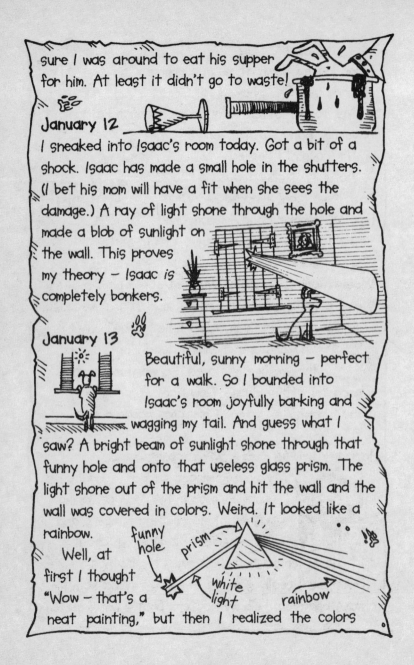

January 13

Beautiful, sunny morning — perfect for a walk. So I bounded into Isaac's room joyfully barking and wagging my tail. And guess what I saw? A bright beam of sunlight shone through that funny hole and onto that useless glass prism. The light shone out of the prism and hit the wall and the wall was covered in colors. Weird. It looked like a rainbow.

Well, at first I thought "Wow — that's a neat painting," but then I realized the colors

funny hole
prism
white light
rainbow

were made by the light. "Maybe that prism has magical powers," I thought.

Then I saw the broad grin on Isaac's face.

"What do you think of the rainbow, Diamond?" he whispered excitedly, pressing his face up close.

"Woof!" I replied. This is usually the best response when Isaac gets worked up about something.

"Bet you'd like to know how I made it?" asked Isaac.

Well, I was wondering and luckily he went on to explain the trick.

"You see, sunlight is made of different colors."

I wagged my tail and looked interested as Isaac continued in a rather breathless voice.

"When the colors in light hit the prism at an angle they all bend or refract by different amounts. So the colors separate out from the white light and you see a rainbow."

Well, all this Science was a bit over my head and anyway I was eager for a walk. Luckily Isaac's mum heard me whining and she took me outside.

Ah – what a relief!

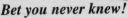

Bet you never knew!

Newton was the first person to describe seven colors in light, but actually there's lots more. Newton liked the idea of seven colors, though, because it reminded him of the seven notes in music. (And if you want to know more about colors check out pages 122-139.)

Blazing a trail

Although Isaac wasn't the first person to make a rainbow using a prism, he was the first to prove colors are part of sunlight and not somehow made by the glass. He did this by shining red light from his "rainbow" through a second prism and finding that it didn't split any further.

RAY OF SUNLIGHT

PRISM 1

LOOK, DIAMOND! THE RED LIGHT WON'T SPLIT ANY FURTHER!

NARROW SLIT IN SCREEN ALLOWS ONLY RED BAND OF RAINBOW THROUGH

PRISM 2

Isaac had blazed a trail in science but his work sparked a blazing argument. He sent an account of it to the Royal Society (that's the club for top scientists founded in 1662) but rival scientist Robert Hooke (1635-1703) claimed that Isaac's experiments didn't work properly. In fact, the glass in Hooke's prism probably wasn't as clear as Newton's so he couldn't get the same results. But as a result of the fight, Newton stopped speaking to Hooke.

Isaac also suffered another kind of blaze. He returned to Cambridge after the plague, but one Sunday he went to church leaving a candle burning in his laboratory. Maybe Diamond wanted to try a few experiments too. Anyway, he jumped on the table, knocked over the candle and started a fire. According to one report, the blaze destroyed all Isaac's notes on light and all his chemistry equipment. I bet poor Diamond ended up in the dog house.

Isaac rewrote his notes from memory. But he didn't publish any of his work until 1704. By this time Hooke was dead so Isaac got the last word on light. Except, of course, it wasn't the last word. Isaac had believed light was made of tiny balls. But there was no way he could see the balls so his idea was a bit of a stab in the dark — ha ha. And within a century a brilliant scientist would see the problem in a different light.

Hall of fame: Thomas Young (1773-1829)
Nationality: British

Young Tom Young was frighteningly clever. He was so brilliant at school that the whole class probably wanted to sit next to him in science tests. He learned to read when he was two. By the time he was six he'd read the Bible — twice. By the time he was 14 he was designing telescopes and microscopes with the help of a friendly teacher. By then he could speak four languages besides English and he decided (no doubt as a bit of light relief) to teach himself eight more.

I'LL LEARN RUSSIAN, POLISH AND CHINESE... THEN I'LL HAVE LUNCH

Tom trained as a doctor but in 1797 his uncle died and left him a fortune. This was good news. Well, not for the uncle, but good news for Tom. At last he could afford to do what he really wanted — lots of science experiments.

Unfortunately, few people got to hear of Tom's discoveries. His articles were so boring that not many people bothered to read them. Not surprising really — Tom was fired from a job at the Royal Institution because his lectures were too dull. (Note: this is unlikely to happen to your teacher. So stop daydreaming and get on with this book.)

In 1803 Tom proved that light takes the form of light waves. This was quite an achievement because as you know light waves are too small to see — 14,000 light waves could stretch across your thumbnail. In fact, the idea of light waves wasn't totally new. It had been put forward in 1690 by Dutch astronomer Christiaan Huygens (1629-1695) who based his suggestion on complex math. But it was Thomas Young who dreamed up the experiment that proved light waves really exist.

Here's how he did it:

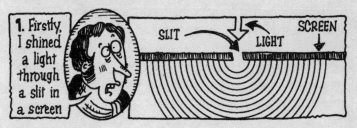

2. The light passed through two slits side by side in a second screen and spread out.

SECOND SCREEN WITH TWO SLITS

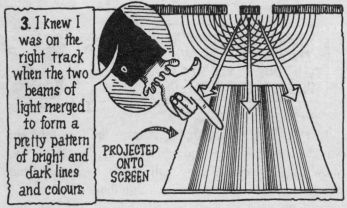

3. I knew I was on the right track when the two beams of light merged to form a pretty pattern of bright and dark lines and colours.

PROJECTED ONTO SCREEN

4. Tom was able to show how this pattern was made by waves of light spreading out from the two slits. The two sets of waves spread out and passed through each other. Where the waves got in each other's way they made shadows – those were the dark lines.

Remember that light contains different colors? Where two light waves only partly blocked each other's way you saw the colors made by the waves that got through. But at the points the two sets of light waves actually managed to pass through one another you saw them both. This made the bright lines. Got all that?

Frightening expressions

One physicist says to another

So who's interfering with the action?

The final, final word?

More evidence built up to show that light took the form of waves and that Huygens and Young were right. For example, in 1818 French physicist Augustin Jean Fresnel (1788-1827) used complex math to show how light waves can produce reflections and refraction. But was light really nothing more than a collection of waves? Was Newton's idea of light just a load of nonsense?

In 1901 German physicist Max Planck (1858-1947) spoiled the party. Planck said light is actually made of blips of energy called "quanta." Max's figures explained how the energy of light can be turned into heat inside a black box. But the only way his calculations added up was if light comes in quanta. These quanta are now called photons.

Four years later a scientific mega-genius used math to prove Planck right. He performed no experiments and used only a pen and notepad for calculations. But he was able to prove that light was made up of photons, but that each blip moves so fast it forms a light wave. This idea was gradually accepted by physicists.

So who was this extraordinary scientist?

Extraordinary Einstein

Albert Einstein is best known for his theories of relativity that he came up with in 1905 and 1915.

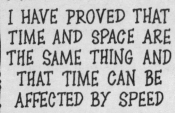

If you haven't a clue what he's talking about, don't worry — you're not alone. There's a good chance that your teacher isn't aware of the finer details either.

Of course, most well-informed teachers can tell you that Einstein was born in Germany, that he made his 1905 discoveries while working in Switzerland, and that in the 1930s he moved to America. But here are five facts they probably don't know about awesome Albert.

1. Einstein got interested in light at the age of 14 when he was daydreaming (no doubt during a particularly boring Science lesson). He imagined he was riding on top of a beam of light.

This was dangerous (that's daydreaming, not riding on — light — as you know, it's impossible to surf on light). In those days, the punishment for not paying attention was a whack across the knuckles with a cane. History doesn't record whether Albert suffered this punishment but he probably did.

2. Einstein was eventually expelled from school. His teacher couldn't stand the sight of him lolling at the back of the class and smiling and not doing any work. But Einstein was a genius and he was more interested in his own studies. (The chances are you won't get away with this excuse.)

3. Some people think that Einstein's discoveries about light were actually made by Mileva Einstein — Albert's first wife. Albert once remarked:

EVERYTHING I HAVE CREATED AND ATTAINED I OWE TO MILEVA

However their son, Hans Albert, explained that although Mileva helped with the math it was Albert who did the scientific thinking. Albert probably meant that having Mileva to look after him gave him the time and confidence to develop his ideas.

4. After Einstein's death doctors removed his brain from inside of his skull and stored it in a box. Their aim was to make it available to researchers into genius. But in fact, the brain looked much the same as anyone else's.

ALBERT EINSTEIN (GENIUS)

ALBERT SHUTTLEWORTH (DIMWIT)

5. At the same time as Einstein's brain was removed, the doctors removed his eyeballs as souvenirs.

Would you want souvenirs like these? Probably not, and if bloodshot eyeballs make you shudder, you might want to close your own eyes before you turn the page.

Because the next chapter is *bulging* with them.

BULGING  EYEBALLS

Here's a really FRIGHTENING thought. Imagine one morning you opened your eyes and saw nothing — just darkness. As black as the darkest night without even a glimmer of starlight. You'd be in a blind panic, wouldn't you? (Or you might think it actually was night and go back to sleep.)

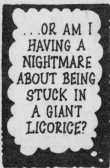

Well, thank goodness for eyeballs. If it weren't for them, you wouldn't be able to see any light at all.

Bulging eyeballs quiz
If you're itching to know more about eyeballs, here's one that's been freshly cut in half. In this quiz each part of the eyeball has a matching fact. All you have to do is match the part of eyeball to the relevant facts.

Eyeball bits and pieces
1. Ciliary muscles
2. Iris
3. Optic nerve
4. Retina with rod and cone cells*

5. Cornea
6. Eyelashes
7. Lens
8. Watery bit
9. Sclera
10. Eye muscles

*By the way, the "cells" are the 60 trillion tiny living jelly-like blobs that make up your body. But you probably knew that already.

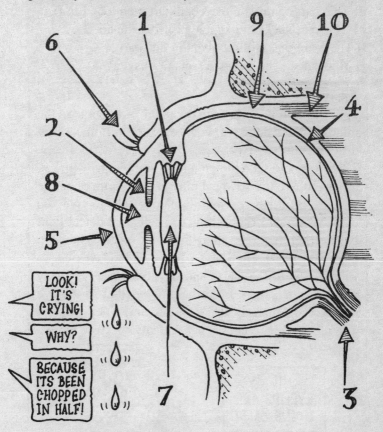

Relevant facts

a) There are 200 of these.

b) This part helps to keep the eyeball in shape.

c) They keep your eyeball from slopping out of its socket.

d) The color of this part stops light from getting through and dazzling you.

e) This part is one square inch (6.5 square cm). Without it you'd see nothing.

f) This part changes shape 100,000 times a day.

g) This part controls the eyeball part mentioned in **f**).

h) This part sucks in oxygen gas from the air.

i) There are one million fibers in this part.

j) You can see the blood vessels in this part.

Answers:

1g) 2d) Light goes through the pupil — the hole in the middle. (The color of your eye doesn't make any difference to what you see.) **3i)** They're nerve fibers. Their job is to take the pattern of light signals picked up by the retina to the brain in the form of nerve signals. **4e)** It has seven million cone cells to give you color vision and 130 million rod cells that detect light but not colors. (For more info. on color vision see page 134.) **5h)** The cornea has no blood vessels to supply it with the sugar and oxygen it needs to stay alive. It gets sugars from the gloopy fluid in the eye and oxygen directly from the air. **6a)** They fall out after about three months, but you always grow more.

AAH! MY EYELIDS ARE GOING BALD!

7f) The lens thickens or lengthens so that light from whatever you are looking at is bent (refracted) and so focused on the retina. That's blinking amazing, isn't it? **8b)** Yes, it's true, you're looking at this page through a pool of watery jelly. **9j)** It's the "white" of your eyeball. When the eyeball is injured or has a disease the blood vessels get inflamed and get bigger. And the eyeball looks red and bloodshot. **10c)** They also swivel the eyeball around to look at things. Your brain coordinates the muscles on each eyeball so they work together. When this doesn't happen you go cross-eyed.

Bet you never knew!

1. The way your retina lets you see light is horribly complicated. When you look at something, photons of light hit the cells in the retina. These cells contain colored chemicals called pigments. The photons spark a series of chemical reactions first in the pigments and then in the cells. These create a nerve signal that travels to the brain. And get this — all this confusing, chaotic chemistry happens more or less instantly. And all the time.

2. So how good are your eyeballs? Are they sharp as needles or a sight for sore eyes? Why not put them through their paces? Your eyeballs should be good enough to spot a coin in the playground at 213 feet (65 meters). Better make sure the playground is empty before trying this experiment, though.

Now for another eyeball test.

Dare you discover . . . how something horrible appears to happen to your hand?

What you need:

One red piece of construction paper

One left hand (Go on, use your own, it won't hurt . . . honest!)

What you do:

1. Roll the paper lengthways into a tube 1 inch (2.5 cm) across.

2. Stand with a window on your right.

3. Put the tube to your right eye. Stare hard with both eyes open.

4. Place your left hand against the left side of the tube with your thumb underneath the tube.

What do you notice?

a) Your hand . . . has disappeared.

b) Aah! A hole has appeared in your hand.

c) Oh no! You have two left hands.

Answer:

b) Your left and your right eyes are seeing different views. Your brain combines them to make a 3-D scene. This is what happens all the time when you look at things, but in this case the scene is a rather horrible illusion.

46

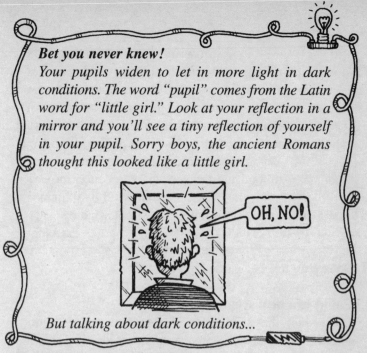

But talking about dark conditions...

Teacher's lunchtime teaser

This teaser works best in a dark, sinister, gloomy corridor (most schools have a few). You'll need a book with very small print. (Try using a boring science book, not this one, obviously.) Knock on the staffroom door. When the door opens smile sweetly and ask:

Enjoy watching your teacher struggling with the tiny print. Then ask them why people can't read in the dark.

Does your teacher know both answers?

Could you be a scientist?
Of course, these important facts about vision didn't
discover themselves. Scientists and doctors had to find
them out by careful investigation. The discovery of how
the lens in your eye focuses light was made by Thomas
Young in 1792 using a real eyeball.

But where did it come from?

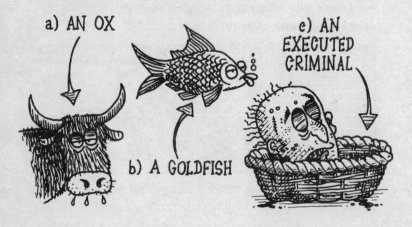

a) AN OX

c) AN
EXECUTED
CRIMINAL

b) A GOLDFISH

Test your teacher

You can liven up a boring swimming lesson by asking this tricky science question. It's sure to make a big splash.

*WHY DOES EVERYTHING APPEAR
BLURRED UNDER WATER?

Answer:

Normally light refracts (that's bends, remember) as it passes through the cornea. This bending happens as light passes from the air into the watery cornea. This helps to bend light on to the retina allowing you to see things in focus.

49

When you're underwater the light is already going through water so it doesn't bend into the cornea. As a result the light isn't so well focused on your retina and things appear blurred.

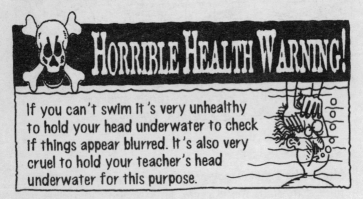

Frightening expressions

An ophthalmologist asks:

Talking about eye problems, take a very close look at this (if you can).

Dear Doc

Each week Dr. Scalpel answers your health questions. This week...

PROBLEMS WITH THE EYEBALLS

Dear Doc,
I'm a soccer referee with TERRIBLE eyesight. I can't always spot when a player is offside. I should explain, Doc, that "offside" means collecting

Continued

a forward pass with no opponents between you and the goal line when the ball is kicked. And it's not allowed. But as I said, I'm not always sure when a player is offside. You see, they move so fast it's very confusing. And when I make the wrong decision the fans call me rude names. It's so hurtful I could cry.
Should I retire?

Mr. I.B. Worried

Dear Mr. Worried
Cheer up – your eyesight is normal. In 1998 eye specialists in Madrid, Spain found that it takes 300 milliseconds for an eye to focus on a moving player. Meanwhile the player might have moved several feet. So it's hard to be sure when a player's offside. Well, Mr. Worried, this embarrassing secret is safe with me and the 200,000 readers of the *Daily Searchlight*.

P.S. Funny how fans can always spot when a player from the opposing team is offside.

Dear Doc
I keep seeing dark dots
in front of my eyes —
am I going dotty?
I.C. Spottes

Dear Mr Spottes
The dots you describe are probably caused by
blood clots on your retina. A larger dark
spot may be caused by damage to your retina.
In both cases you should see a doctor. I'm
sure they'll spot the problem.

Dear Doc
My eyesight is gradually
disappearing round the edges of
my field of vision. When I look
at a light I see a blurred
halo around it. "Halo, halo,
halo," I said to
myself — I must be
seeing things. What
do you think?

Mrs N.D. Dark

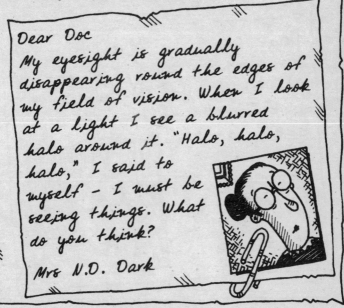

Dear Mrs. Dark

You sound like you might have glaucoma. The watery gloop in your eyeball is produced behind your iris. For reasons we doctors don't understand, you can make too much gloop. It builds up inside your eyeball pressing outwards until it squeezes your optic nerve — that's the nerve that takes signals from your retina to your brain. This reduces vision and causes blindness. But don't panic! You can take drops to cut the amount of gloop your eye makes and relieve the pressure on your nerve.

That's a relief — eh?

Dear Doc

Please help me - I think I'm going blind. My eyesight is blurred and dim. I keep seeing double. What's happening to me?

Ms. Rabble

Dear Ms. Rabble

You could have a cataract. A build up of fluid in the lens leads to chemical changes that cause a cloudy area. Seeing double happens when two cloudy areas refract light from the same object. Fortunately the cataract can be removed in a simple operation.

P.S. One traditional remedy for cataracts was to plop a warm drop of pee (or urine, as we doctors call it) into the eye. Don't try this — it's useless and may cause infection.

> **DON'T MISS NEXT WEEK.** It 'snot' much fun having problems with your nostrils. **Dear Doc** looks into noses.

There are lots of possible causes for cataracts, including damage to the lens after being outside too much under the huge, sizzling, blinding solar nuclear explosion in the sky.

The what?

The sun, of course.

It's time to put on those shades and turn the page.

55

SIZZLING SUNSHINE

We're all lucky people. Every day we get hours and hours of free sunshine. Well, OK, that's true for California and it's not quite so true if you're snowed up in Siberia. But even when the weather's nasty — cheer up — the sun's shining up there above the clouds, providing warmth and light. And all for free!

But the sun is more than a big light bulb in the sky. The whole future of life on Earth depends on the sun. This fact is so basic even aliens know about it.

R E P O R T   B Y

OddblOb the Blurb

▶ **MISSION:** Inter-planetary probe of medium-sized star system with a star known locally as the sun.

GALAXY CO-ORDINATES: 0001.1100.0011100.0

MAP:

ALIEN DRIBBLE   MARS

EARTH

VENUS

SUN   MERCURY   (SENSORS REVEAL AT LEAST FIVE OUTER PLANETS)

INTELLIGENT LIFE ◄ • • • • • • • • • • •

A species known as
humanoids are very
abundant on Planet Earth.
We have captured a specially
trained humanoid known as a
"science teacher" for further

Science teacher – emitted
squeaky sound like,
"ARR-YOR-AN-ALEEE-EN!"

research. The names given to planets in this report are
names used by the humanoid.

STAR STATUS ◄ • • • • • • • • • • • •

The sun is in the middle of its life. It is 4.5 billion
years old. The center is 27,000,000° F (14,000,000° C).
Light photons are produced by atoms as they are
fused together. Just like any other star of this
type, really.

PLANET EARTH ◄ • • • • • • • • • • •

This planet is the only one suitable for life. Life on
planet Earth depends on light from the sun.

PLANTS – GREEN NON-
MOVING LIFE FORMS.
PLANTS USE ENERGY
FROM SUNLIGHT TO TURN
WATER AND CARBON
DIOXIDE GAS FROM AIR
INTO FOOD.

HUMANOIDS EAT
ANIMALS AND PLANTS.

ANIMALS – MOBILE
LIFE FORMS THAT
EAT PLANTS OR
OTHER ANIMALS.

Sensors report that without the sun there would be
no plants, no animals and humanoids would be
missing out on their intake of nutritive chemicals
otherwise known as lunch.

INVASION POTENTIAL ◀ • • • • • • • • • • • • •

Planet Earth is suitable for invasion – but from
our study of the science teacher we have
established that humans spend
much of their time communicating
boring information. Life on Earth
may prove unbearably dull for
higher forms of intelligence such
as Blurbs. So we have erased the
humanoid's memory of our visit
and put him back where we
found him.

ZONK!...now
where was I...ah
yes, your science
homework, Smith...

Awesome eclipses

One dramatic effect of the sun is called an eclipse. This
is caused by the moon getting in the way of the sun's
light so that its shadow falls on the Earth.

SHADOW OF MOON
MOON
EARTH
SUNLIGHT
SUN
ARGH! IT'S UNBEARABLY DULL!
THE HUMANOIDS AGREE WITH US, ODDBLOB!

Oh, so you knew that? Well, in the past many people
didn't — so they made up stories and performed rituals
to make sense of what was going on.

1. An eclipse can be frightening. If you don't know what's happening, it looks like the moon is swallowing the sun. According to ancient Greek writer Thucydides (460-400 B.C.) an eclipse halted a battle in Persia in the sixth century B.C. The two armies drew back and agreed to go on with the battle after a month, when any bad magical effects had worn off.

2. In ancient China people thought a dragon was eating the sun and banged gongs or pans to scare the monster away.

3. The native peoples of North America fired flaming arrows at the sky in a bid to re-light the sun.

4. The Pampas tribes of South America believed the moon goddess was darkened in an eclipse with her own blood drawn by savage dogs. Of course, they were barking up the wrong tree.

5. Some Tartar tribes in Asia believed the sun and moon were swallowed up by a blood-sucking vampire from a distant star.

6. In many countries people thought (wrongly) that diseases spread during eclipses. The Yukon tribes of Alaska covered their pots and pans during eclipses for this reason. A terrible outbreak of influenza that claimed thousands of victims in South America in 1918 was blamed by some on an eclipse.

Dare you discover . . . how to observe an eclipse?

Eclipses of the sun are fairly rare. There are often less than five a year — so chances are, you won't be able to see one from your own backyard. To see one you might have to travel to far-flung places like the North Pole. Well, when you get there, here's a way to watch the eclipse without hurting your eyes.

Note: If there aren't any eclipses coming up you can always use this method to look at the sun safely. You can try it at home in a shaft of bright sunlight.

What you need:
The sun
A sheet of cardboard with a pin hole in the centre. (Make sure the hole is perfectly round and open.)
A sheet of smooth paper
A tape measure

What you do:
1. Stand with your back to the sun.
2. Hold the cardboard so light from the sun shines through the hole on to the paper. The second sheet should be about three feet from the first.
3. You should see an image of the sun about 0.4 inches (one cm) across.

URGENT HORRIBLE HEALTH WARNING!

Staring at the sun even during an eclipse is dangerous. You need to wear special protective glasses, otherwise the bright light kills cells in your retina and lens. This can cause cataracts and blindness. In fact, gazing at any really bright light can be harmful. Welders who don't use protective goggles get "arc eye" and go blind for a while – or even for ever. So you'd be blind stupid to risk it.

A snap decision

If you think the dangers of observing an eclipse sound rather frightening, spare a thought for Warren de la Rue (1815-1889). In 1860 top astronomer Sir John Herschel

(1792-1871) asked this intrepid British photographer to travel to Rivabellosa in Spain to photograph an eclipse and prove a scientific fact.

"So Warren got a nice suntan and took a few vacation pictures. What's so risky about that?" I hear you ask.

Well, in 1860 cameras were in their infancy and travel was a bit more primitive. So this was quite an undertaking. Here's what Warren's letters home might have looked like:

July 17, 1860
To Sir John Herschel
Kew Observatory, England

SPEW!

Dear Sir John,
Here I am at Rivabellosa and what a terrible journey it's been! I was seasick and throwing up during the voyage to Spain. And the hassle of getting the equipment to the village! As you know, the combined camera and telescope we're going to use is almost as tall as me and weighs a few tons. The village is hundreds of miles from the sea. And the roads here are tracks. I'm covered in dust and I had to spend a fortune hiring smelly carts.

Is this really the best place to see the eclipse? Wasn't there anywhere else nearer?

Oh well, we're here now. I'll write soon.

Yours wearily,

← Me

Warren

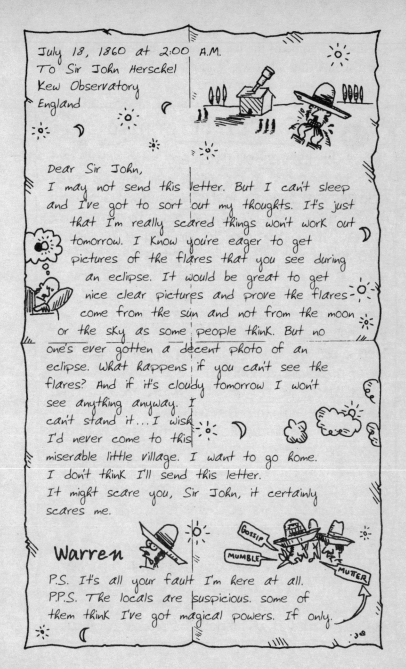

July 18, 1860 at 2:00 A.M.
To Sir John Herschel
Kew Observatory
England

Dear Sir John,

I may not send this letter. But I can't sleep and I've got to sort out my thoughts. It's just that I'm really scared things won't work out tomorrow. I know you're eager to get pictures of the flares that you see during an eclipse. It would be great to get nice clear pictures and prove the flares come from the sun and not from the moon or the sky as some people think. But no one's ever gotten a decent photo of an eclipse. What happens if you can't see the flares? And if it's cloudy tomorrow I won't see anything anyway. I can't stand it... I wish I'd never come to this miserable little village. I want to go home. I don't think I'll send this letter. It might scare you, Sir John, it certainly scares me.

Warren

P.S. It's all your fault I'm here at all.
P.P.S. The locals are suspicious. some of them think I've got magical powers. If only.

GOSSIP
MUMBLE
MUTTER

Meanwhile some of the people of Rivabellosa must have been wondering what was going on. Here's how events might have appeared to a young boy.

THE ECLIPSE BY PEDRO

Our teacher told us all about the eclipse. But the old people in our village said it would bring sickness and disaster. That's what Grandpa thought. He said the sweaty Englishman had a magic machine to make the sun go dark for as long as he wished.

The day of the eclipse was bright and sunny. I went up the hill with Grandpa to get a good view. Grandpa was still grumbling and saying no good will come of it. There were crowds of people. The Englishman had his machine set up — I could see the end of it sticking out the top of a shed like a giant gun.

Just before the eclipse, we saw the moon getting close to the sun. Then a horrible dark shadow appeared in the distance. It was the shadow of the moon. The darkness swept over the hills like a thunderstorm. Everything went grey. All the flowers closed up and birds started snoozing in the trees. It was just like evening so I started yawning.

"Bored already?" snapped Grandpa.

Then things got scary.   Grandpa →

Little by little the sun was swallowed up by the moon until all you could see was a black glowing circle. Suddenly my hair stood on end — I was seriously worried. It was dark. The stars had come out.

Maybe Grandpa was right.

Perhaps the sun had gone for ever.

I grabbed hold of his hand.

Meanwhile the Englishman was acting crazy. Shouting at his assistants and disappearing into the shed to work his giant machine. We heard him muttering things to himself.

"He's saying spells," whispered Grandpa.

So Grandpa got down on to his bony knees and started reciting prayers. But there was no sign of the sun.

Where was it?

The minutes dragged by...

Just then a bright bead of light appeared. It looked like a diamond ring around the dark moon. Everyone cheered. I found myself dancing up and down.

"It's a miracle!" cried Grandpa, struggling to his feet.

It began to get light. Soon the sun was shining again in the blue sky. The eclipse was scary but amazing. No one got ill, nothing terrible happened. I wish we had an eclipse every week. It's much better than listening to Grandpa strumming his guitar and singing awful old songs.

July 18, 1860 at 4:00 p.m.
To Sir John Herschel
Kew Observatory, England

Dear Sir John,
It's over and I'm shattered. Completely drained. Well, I tried. I took 35 shots

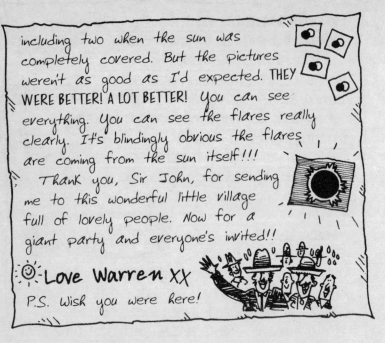

including two when the sun was completely covered. But the pictures weren't as good as I'd expected. THEY WERE BETTER! A LOT BETTER! You can see everything. You can see the flares really clearly. It's blindingly obvious the flares are coming from the sun itself!!!

Thank you, Sir John, for sending me to this wonderful little village full of lovely people. Now for a giant party and everyone's invited!!

Love Warren xx

P.S. Wish you were here!

A scientist writes

Spanish scientist Father Angelo Secchi (1818-1878) also took a series of photos of the eclipse. Father Secchi was over 248 miles (400 km) to the southeast but the flares in his pictures matched the ones taken by De La Rue. This was the final proof that the flares had definitely come from the sun.

Dark secrets

It gets dark during an eclipse because the moon casts its shadow over the Earth. You get a shadow any time a solid object blocks light. (That's how the climber on the Brocken Mountain made the "ghost.") Something that blocks light is described as opaque. And you can use an opaque shape to make horrible shadows.

Dare you discover . . . what lurks in the shadows?

What you need:
A pencil
A pair of scissors
A piece of black cardboard. You can always paint a white piece of cardboard black.
A piece of wire
Sticky tape
A small, bright flashlight
A room with light walls

What you do:
1. Draw and cut out a monster shape.
2. Tape the wire to the bottom of the shape to make a handle.
3. Wait until it gets dark. Close the curtains and switch on your flashlight. Place the flashlight about 9.8 feet (three meters) from the wall.
4. Hold the wire so the shape is between the light and the wall. You can make great sinister shadows. Hold on, sorry to spoil things, but this is a serious scientific experiment, after all. So. . .

What do you notice?

a) You moved the shape toward the wall and away from the flashlight. The shadow on the wall got larger.

b) When the shape is closer to the light it blocks more light. This throws a larger shadow on the wall.

c) As you moved the flashlight the shadow began to move in the opposite direction. Help — it's alive!

 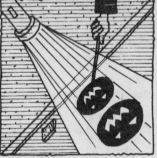

Answer:

b) When the shape is closer to the light, it blocks more light. This throws a larger shadow on the wall. The larger shadow has more of a blurred edge than the smaller one. This is because some light from the edges of the flashlight can still shine past the edges of the shape, but not enough to give a sharp edge to the shadow.

Strange starlight

Of course, astronomers aren't just interested in sunlight. They're also very excited by the topic of starlight. If you have secret ambitions to be an astronomer you might like to train your telescope on this next bit.

The stars are a long way away. A very long way away. You'll remember that sunlight takes about eight and half minutes to reach us. But that's a blink of an eye for starlight. Even the light of our next door neighbor star Alpha Centauri takes four years to arrive. But that's nothing. If you live in the northern part of the world the most distant object you'll see is the Andromeda galaxy. The photons from this star cluster started out 2.2 million years before you were born. And you thought waiting for the school bus took forever.

Astronomers are interested in starlight because without it they wouldn't be able to see stars. And by studying the color of the light they can work out the surface temperature of the star. For example, a bluish white star is a sizzling 54,000°F (30,000°C) and a red star is a nice cool 3,600°F (2,000°C). (OK, that's cool by star standards — the hottest temperatures on Earth include

California's Death Valley, which reached 120°F (49°C) in 1917. Any hotter than that here and it would be Death Valley for the human race.)

The brightness of a star can also be used mathematically to work out its distance from Earth. This brilliant fact was noted by U.S. astronomer Henrietta Leavitt (1868-1921).

Bet you never knew!
Stars are colored. It's true! The reason they seem white to us is that most stars are very dim. They only give your eye about 500 photons a second. This means that we can only see them with our dim-light-detecting rod cells. And the rod cells can't see colors, can they?

Could you be an astronomer?
You've probably heard the rhyme:

Twinkle, twinkle little star
How I wonder what you are!

Next time you gaze at a star consider this puzzle:
Why do stars twinkle?

a) Because their light flashes on and off.

b) Because the starlight is refracted (bent) by gusts of wind.

c) Because fast-moving clouds keep blocking the light.

Answer:

b) As the wind blows, the atoms that make up air may get more crowded together in one area than another. As light passes through this area it refracts (bends) producing a twinkling effect. In fact, moonlight does this too but because the moon appears bigger to us you don't notice it twinkling around the edges.

Bet you never knew!
If you want to spot stars it helps if you live a long way away from the neighbors. In built-up areas the night sky often glows with the light of streetlights and shop signs reflecting off water droplets and dust in the air. This spoils the view of the twinkling stars.

But if lights are bad news for astronomers they're very good news for small, frightened kids who are scared of the dark. So if you're reading this at dusk, maybe you'd better turn on the light before you switch to the next chapter.

It will brighten you . . . and frighten you.

FRIGHTENING LIGHTING

This is a chapter about things that glow in the dark. And not all of them are light bulbs. Yep — long before anyone flicked a light switch, before even some bright spark invented fire, strange unearthly lights flickered in the darkness.

Intrigued? Let's bring the FRIGHTENING facts to light.

Frightening light fact file

NAME: Bioluminescence

THE BASIC FACTS: 1. Certain living creatures can produce light.

2. Their bodies make a chemical called luciferin and another called luciferase.

3. Luciferin combines with oxygen from the creatures blood and gives out light. Luciferase speeds up this chemical reaction.

THE FRIGHTENING DETAILS: Some bacteria do this. Some fish (see below) eat the bacteria. The bacteria remain alive and make light in the fish's skin.

'GLO' AWAY, YOU'RE UGLY!

THE GLOW IN THE DARK
ZOO

Welcome to the world's first zoo where the animals provide the lighting...

Comb jelly

Jelly-fish-like creature 9.8–11.8 inches (25–30 cm) long.

FOUND IN: Pacific and Atlantic Oceans.

LIGHT IS USED FOR: scaring off attackers.

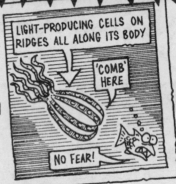

LIGHT-PRODUCING CELLS ON RIDGES ALL ALONG ITS BODY

'COMB' HERE

NO FEAR!

Deep sea angler fish

FOUND IN: deep oceans throughout the world

LIGHT IS USED FOR: catching other fish

WORM-LIKE BLOB (FILLED WITH GLOWING BACTERIA) ON THE END OF A LINE LURES SMALLER FISH TO THEIR DOOM.

HMMM, INTERESTING!

Fire flies and glow-worms

FOUND IN: fireflies live in North America and glowworms live in Europe. Actually they're both varieties of beetle.

PHWOAR! HE'S NICE!

FIRE FLY

LIGHT IS USED FOR: signaling for a mate.

HERE I AM, BOYS!

Both insects have glowing lights on their bottoms. (Imagine you had one of these — you'd never need a rear bike light.)

GLOW-WORM

Luminous plankton

Tiny creatures often less than 0.04 inches (1 mm) long called copepods. The plankton also include plants called dinoflagellates.

COPEPOD

FOUND IN: every ocean especially where the water is rich in minerals.

LIGHT IS USED FOR: scaring away attackers. Ship toilets are often flushed with seawater — if the plankton are present they make your toilet glow in the dark. (Is this why they call it a "flash in the pan"?)

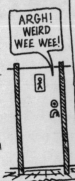

ARGH! WEIRD WEE WEE!

DINOFLAGELLATE

But there are other kinds of light around and these are not made by animals. Not living ones, anyway.

Could you be a scientist?
It's 200 years ago. You're walking home and you bravely decide to take a short cut through the graveyard. It's very dark — you're scared . . . and suddenly you see an eerie glow. What's causing it?
a) It's a ghost. Yikes, I'm out of here.
b) It's a mass of glow-worms feeding off rotting vegetation.
c) It's gases from a rotting body.

Answer:
c) Before new cemeteries were opened up in Victorian times many old churchyards became filled up. Dead bodies were buried one on top of the other under a shallow layer of soil. Germs inside the rotting bodies made methane and phosphine gas. As the gases reached the surface they often caught fire as a result of chemical reactions with oxygen in the air. The result was a pale blue glow that was called a will o' the wisp.

Awful artificial light

We take it for granted that by flicking a switch we can have light whenever we want. It's a part of every day life and without it you wouldn't be able to see this page, or even see to do homework (that would be tragic!). But just imagine you lived a few hundred years before there were light bulbs. Don't worry, you didn't have to use the glowing gas from a dead body. But the alternatives were almost as frightening.

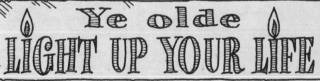

Ye olde LIGHT UP YOUR LIFE
home shopping catalogue

ROMANTIC CANDLES

Why not light your home with a genuine olde worlde candle as used by people since ancient Egyptian times. Wow, what a dazzling choice!

NOW WE HAVE TO WAIT 3500 YEARS FOR SOMEONE TO INVENT MATCHES

CONTINUED...

Traditional tallow candle

▷ Made with boiled up fat from around the kidneys of a dead cow, sheep or horse.

THE SMALL PRINT: Tallow candles are smelly and greasy. They go out easily and the smell is so bad that in parts of the West Indies the candles are lit to keep the bugs at bay.

WE'VE RUN OUT OF TALLOW CANDLES, WIFE.

Heat from the flame melts the fat.

▷ Beeswax – the de-luxe alternative. Genuine waxy stuff squirted from the bodies of bees and built up to make chambers for their grubs to live in.

The flame burns the fat

The wick sucks up the fat.

Modern paraffin candle

▷ Made from oil.

▷ Burns with a nice bright flame

THE SMALL PRINT: It's still a fire hazard and melted wax can drip everywhere and make a mess. Oh, and the light can become dim and flickering if you don't trim the wick.

SORRY MOM, IT'S MADE A MESS...

GRRR, I'LL GIVE YOU WAX!

THE AMAZING ARC-LIGHT

Invented by British scientist Sir Humphrey Davy (1778-1829) in 1808

WELL, CANDLES WENT OUT WITH THE ARK

▷ Electric current jumps across the gap between two carbon rods. (Make sure there's a constant gap between two carbon rods as the light burns, otherwise the rods will melt or the light will fizzle out.)

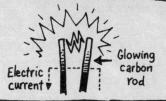

Electric current

Glowing carbon rod

THE SMALL PRINT: This light is a fire hazard. And it could blind you because it's brighter than 4,000 candles. The only practical use anyone ever found for it was in the Dungeness lighthouse. So unless your house happens to be a lighthouse it's probably not such a good idea.

TURN IT OFF!

GASLIGHT

Flame made by burning coal gas

As invented by Scottish inventor William Murdock (1754-1839

UH — I'M JUST WARMING THE POT, MOM. . .

GRRR!

after an experiment in 1792 involving heating coal in his mom's teapot.

Handy tap to turn the gas on or off

THE SMALL PRINT: You need pipes all over your house to carry the gas. And the gas is poisonous and can blow up your home. And even when it works the flame is smoky and smelly.

MARVELOUS MODERN LIGHTS

Nowadays things are looking much brighter. Go to any street and you'll probably see sodium or mercury street lights. These work in roughly the same way.

An electric current passes through the tube. Atoms in the gas take in energy and give out light.

Something else passing through a tube

Brilliant bulbs

One invention put the others in the shade. The light bulb. And as every American knows, the light bulb was invented by U.S. inventor Thomas A. Edison (1847-1931). And every well-informed Briton knows the light bulb was invented by British inventor Joseph Swan (1828-1914). So what's the truth?

Read on and find out.

Thomas A. Edison's diary

I've got this real smart idea for a new kind of light. All you do is send an electric current through a thin wire. This slows down the flow of electricity. The electric current drags along making the wire heat up and you get light. Simple but brilliant – like most of my inventions.

Hmm – need to pump out the air otherwise the thin wire will catch fire when you heat it up. You can't get fire without air – can you?

THIN WIRE

AIR IS MAKING THIN WIRE CATCH FIRE

ELECTRICITY

THE DAILY SUN

Septermber 1, 1878

Let there be light!

Brilliant inventor Thomas Edison is set to light up the world by inventing the light bulb. Already gas lighting company shares are plummeting at the prospect. And Edison hasn't even built a single bulb yet! But whiz-kid Edison is already famous for inventing the phonograph. (That's the new-fangled machine you can use to play music on.)

MR. T. EDISON

And now he's getting on with a bit of light work!

January 21, 1879

If only I could make this light work. One day there could be a light bulb in every home. There might even be two in every home. I could become seriously rich. But only if everything goes to plan. I've hurt my eyes staring at the light bulbs . . . before they burnt out. Work is getting harder.

Those carbon filaments sure can burn. Seems my pumps aren't good enough to get all the air out of the bulbs. So I tried platinum wires instead – but they kept melting. Then I made a switch to cut the power if the platinum gets too hot but the light keeps flickering. Oh well – back to the drawing board. As I like to say, "inventing is 99 per cent perspiration and only 1 per cent inspiration".

April 1, 1879   99%

Did I say perspiration? Well, I'm in a cold sweat just now. To be precise, I'm at my wit's end. We've tried thousands of materials – rubber, fishing line, wood and now in desperation we're trying human hair. Two of my assistants volunteered to provide the hair. John Kruesli's got a big bushy beard and J.V. Mackenzie's got wiry sideburns.

J.K.   J.V.M.

My staff are all excited and are even betting which hair will last longest without burning.

A few hours later...

Mackenzie's hair is still producing light! Hold on - looks like the electric current's been turned down and the bulb's too dim to be any use. RATS, I figure someone cheated to win the bets. I can't stand these failures - I should never have allowed the papers to print all that rubbish. Maybe I'll never solve this puzzle and go down in history as a dim failure.

DIM!

DIM!

October 17, 1879

I was sitting in the office last night when a bright light bulb seemed to flash in my head. "Oh no - not another light bulb!" I moaned. Then I realized I was having A BRAINWAVE - that's what I mean by INSPIRATION. I thought burnt cotton thread that's turned into carbon might be the answer. Yeah - the magic material has to be carbon. After all, carbon only melts at really high temperatures of about 6332°F (3500°C). And now that I've taken delivery of better air pumps the carbon shouldn't burn up. And . . . well, I just have a hunch about cotton thread.

BUT WILL IT WORK? ? ? ? ? ? ?

October 21, 1879

I could cry. I've been working non-stop for days trying to make a cotton thread filament. Each one takes hours. But they keep breaking at the last moment. They're so thin and fragile. Oh well, here's number three. My heart's in my mouth and I'm switching on the new light bulb. It's burning . . . but for how long?

Gnash!

Chew!

Keep burning . . . please.

← No 3

October 22, 1879

It kept on burning. And burning. I didn't sleep last night. I watched it for every minute of the 13 hours and 30 minutes it stayed lit.

It works! I've done it. I'VE DONE IT!

I could weep with excitement and if I was a bit younger I'd be turning cartwheels. I've cracked the light bulb! No, not cracked the glass - I mean cracked the problem of how to make the light bulb stay alight. After 5,999 failures. YES!

NOW FOR A BLAZE OF PUBLICITY!!!

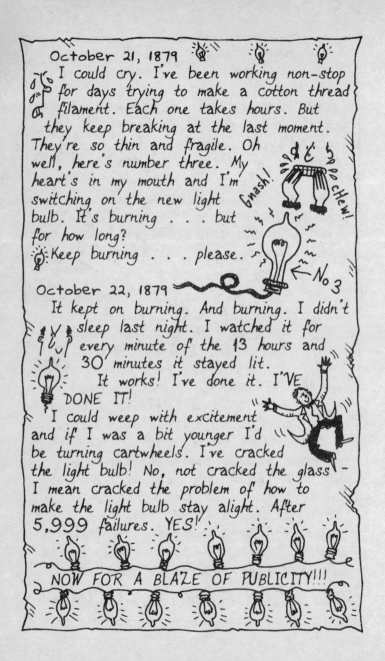

THE DAILY SUN

December 31, 1879

Blaze of glory!

Heroic inventor Thomas A. Edison glowed with pride as he showed off his new invention.

Thousands of people watched him light up the whole town with 3,000 newly-invented light bulbs. Each one looks llike a globe of sunshine. No more will people huddle in the dark afraid of the shadows. Thomas Edison is a shining example to the whole nation! It's such a pity that 14 of the new light bulbs have already been stolen.

January 1, 1880
Terrible news. I've read that a British inventor Joseph Swan claims he invented the light bulb. And he's using carbon fibers, just like me. I'm gnashing my teeth in rage. He says he's been working on it for 25 years. A likely story. He must be an impostor so I'll sue him in J.S. the courts for taking my invention. That's what I'll do - yep, sue the pants off of him!

my bulb

Swan's blasted bulb

But the British courts found that Swan had indeed been making light bulbs before Edison. Swan was a talented chemist whose inventions included artificial silk. He had finally made a successful carbon filament bulb in February 1879. But he didn't patent the invention because he thought people would copy it anyway.

If you were Thomas Edison what would you do next?
a) Pay Swan $1,000,000 to stop making light bulbs.
b) Try to sell cheaper light bulbs than Swan and drive him out of business.
c) Offer to join forces with Swan.

Test your teacher

Here's your chance to put your teacher under the spotlight. Ask them who invented the light bulb. If they know anything they'll say either Thomas Edison or Joseph Swan — or even both. Shake your head sadly and say:

As so often happens in science, the answer gets more complicated the more you find out. Several inventors made carbon filament lights before Swan and Edison. For example, Scottish inventor James Bowman Lindsay made one in 1835. But he didn't tell many people about it. Apparently, he didn't think there would be money in the new invention. And anyway, scientists have continued to improve on Edison's original design. Yes, it really does take quite a few scientists to invent a light bulb.

A brighter idea

A modern light bulb uses a coiled tungsten metal filament surrounded by argon — a harmless gas found in the air.

Modern heat resistant tungsten wires were developed by American William D. Coolidge (1873-1975) (yes, he really did live to be 102). The idea of using a gas in the bulb came from another American, Irving Langmuir (1881-1957).

Bet you never knew!
Light bulbs save lives. Nowadays many lighthouses use electric light from powerful bulbs to warn ships away from rocks. Each lighthouse has its own pattern of flashes so that sailors can work out where they are in the dark.

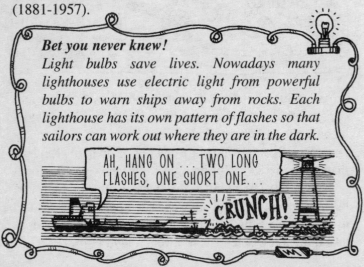

Of course, you'll find bulbs in lots of other places — you might even own a few yourself. Like in your bike lights or your flashlight.

Take a closer look at any of them and you'll find another amazing light gadget. What is it? A mirror, of course, and it's there to reflect the light from the bulb outwards in the direction you want it to go in. And oddly enough, you'll find quite a few mirrors in the next frightening chapter.

FRIGHTENING REFLECTIONS

What's hard, and so shiny you can see your face in it?

No, it's NOT your teacher's bald head.

It's a mirror. When light hits a mirror an amazing thing happens. Light seems to bounce off it to form an image that we call a reflection. Oh, so you knew that already? Well, get this — reflections are unbelievably important to light science. And they pop up in the most unlikely places.

Why not reflect on this quiz for a moment?

Spot the reflection quiz

Reflections can help:

1. Road signs glow in the dark. TRUE/FALSE

2. Clouds glow in the sky. TRUE/FALSE

3. A TV show picture. TRUE/FALSE

4. A shellfish see. TRUE/FALSE

5. A doctor peer inside your eyeball. TRUE/FALSE

6. A mirage appear. TRUE/FALSE

7. Astronomers detect a black hole in space. TRUE/FALSE

8. The snow blind you. TRUE/FALSE

9. A surgeon peer inside your body without cutting you open. TRUE/FALSE

Answers:

1. TRUE. You can find tiny mirrors in road signs and in road studs. The mirrors reflect car headlights. **2. TRUE.** Clouds reflect sunlight. That's what makes them bright and glowing. Thunderclouds appear dark and gloomy from the ground because they are thicker than ordinary clouds and reflect most of the sunlight upwards. Clouds that glow at night do so because they are high enough in the sky to still catch the sunlight. **3. FALSE.** There are no mirrors inside a TV set. **4. TRUE.** Scallops are a type of shellfish with tiny mirrors in their eyes. Each eye has a shiny layer of crystals that reflect light onto cells inside the eye. A scientist made this discovery while looking through a microscope at the shellfish. He saw his own face reflected in the creature's 100 gruesome eyes. **5. TRUE.** A doctor uses an ophthalmoscope to peer inside your eyeball. This instrument shines a light on to a curved mirror that focuses the light beam into your eyeball. The doctor then peers through a hole in the middle of the mirror to inspect your nerves and blood vessels. **6. FALSE.** Mirages are caused by refraction. (Just to remind you, refraction is bent light.) **7. FALSE.** Light can't escape from a black hole (that's why they're black). So you can't spot one with a mirror. **8. TRUE.** Snow reflects light so well that you can be blinded by staring at it for too long in bright sunlight. That's why skiers wear protective goggles. **9. TRUE.** The tube is called an endoscope and it's basically two bundles of optical fibers. One bundle takes light from a light source at one end into the body — just imagine sticking a flashlight down your throat. The surgeon looks through the other bundle to get a close-up of your innards. And speaking of optical fibers. . . .

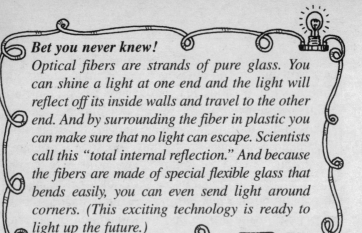

Bet you never knew!

Optical fibers are strands of pure glass. You can shine a light at one end and the light will reflect off its inside walls and travel to the other end. And by surrounding the fiber in plastic you can make sure that no light can escape. Scientists call this "total internal reflection." And because the fibers are made of special flexible glass that bends easily, you can even send light around corners. (This exciting technology is ready to light up the future.)

All right, that's what reflections can do. But how do you make reflections to begin with?

Frightening light fact file

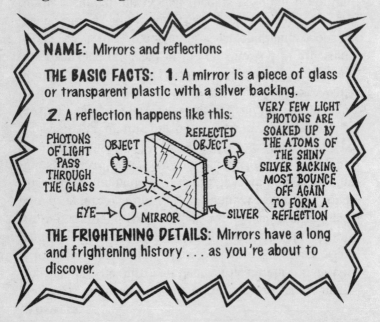

NAME: Mirrors and reflections

THE BASIC FACTS: 1. A mirror is a piece of glass or transparent plastic with a silver backing.

2. A reflection happens like this:

PHOTONS OF LIGHT PASS THROUGH THE GLASS

OBJECT

REFLECTED OBJECT

VERY FEW LIGHT PHOTONS ARE SOAKED UP BY THE ATOMS OF THE SHINY SILVER BACKING. MOST BOUNCE OFF AGAIN TO FORM A REFLECTION

EYE → MIRROR

SILVER

THE FRIGHTENING DETAILS: Mirrors have a long and frightening history . . . as you're about to discover.

Murderous mirrors

• Early people realized that shiny surfaces were great for seeing yourself in. Very handy for helping you brush your hair properly or spot an embarrassing boogie in your nostril.

• In ancient Egypt all sorts of things were used as mirrors including polished metal, wet slates, and bowls of water. But none of them was smooth enough to give a clear, bright image. (In order to see your reflection you need a smooth surface so the photons reflect back together — remember?)

• By the time the Romans came along mirrors were much improved. The Romans used glass to make mirrors with a thin backing of tin. Unfortunately, this invention was to cause a few heated moments. According to legend the Greek scientist Archimedes (287-212 BC) used a bank of mirrors to burn Roman ships that were attacking his home city.

Every mirror reflected sunlight onto a single point on the ship. The wood heated up and burst into flames. This is scientifically possible although there's no proof it happened.

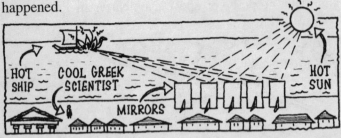

HOT SHIP — COOL GREEK SCIENTIST — MIRRORS — HOT SUN

• In the Middle Ages Venice made the finest mirrors in the world. Venetians had learned to use a mixture of mercury and tin for the backing that was easy to work without heating. This mixture was top secret. A special island was set aside for this work but the mercury was poisonous and many workers died or were driven mad by it. Nevertheless, they were forbidden to pass on the secret on pain of death.

THIS SECRET IS DEADLY. IT'S DEATH IF WE TALK ABOUT IT AND DEATH IF WE DON'T

• Somehow by the 1670s the secret had spread to France and then across Europe. In 1840, German chemist Justus von Liebig (1803-1873) figured out how to put silver backing on a mirror using heated silver nitrate and other chemicals. And this method is still in use.

• Meanwhile the Chinese had been making excellent mirrors from polished metal for over 2,000 years. Some of these mirrors were called "magic mirrors." Can you solve the riddle of their amazing powers?

Could you be a scientist?
You shine a light on a magic mirror. The polished bronze surface reflects back the light on the screen together with a pattern.

But there is no pattern on the surface of the mirror itself. So what causes this strange effect? Only the makers knew the secret. Western and Chinese scientists had been baffled for years. Some Chinese thinkers believed that there was an invisible pattern etched on the front of the mirror that showed up in the reflection.

How would you explain the mirrors?
a) The Chinese thinkers were right. There was a faint pattern on the mirror's surface.
b) The mirrors gave out X-rays that revealed a hidden pattern under the surface.
c) There was a hidden pattern on the back of the mirror that was somehow being reflected from the front.

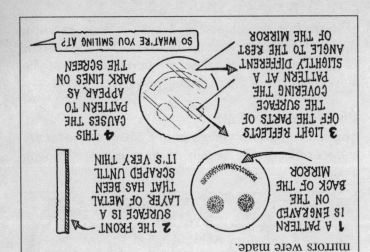

Answer:

c) The first westerners to find the answer were two British physicists, W.E. Ayrton and J. Perry. In the 1890s they were allowed to visit workshops where the mirrors were made.

1 A PATTERN IS ENGRAVED ON THE BACK OF THE MIRROR

2 THE FRONT SURFACE IS A LAYER OF METAL THAT HAS BEEN SCRAPED UNTIL IT'S VERY THIN

3 LIGHT REFLECTS OFF THE PARTS OF THE SURFACE COVERING THE PATTERN AT A SLIGHTLY DIFFERENT ANGLE TO THE REST OF THE MIRROR

4 THIS CAUSES THE PATTERN TO APPEAR AS DARK LINES ON THE SCREEN

SO WHAT'RE YOU SMILING AT?

The pattern appears as dark lines on the screen.

Bet you never knew!

In the Middle Ages people believed they could see the future by staring at a shiny surface such as a mirror. This practice was known as scrying — it's the origin of the traditional fortune teller's crystal ball. Other shiny surfaces used were bowls of water or blood.

YOU WILL CROSS THE SEA IN A LARGE BLOOD VESSEL.

And talking about the bad old days...

Teacher's lunchtime teaser

When your grandparents were young, cruel parents and teachers sometimes forced children to shine their shoes until they could see their faces in them. Here's your chance to get a belated revenge. Knock politely on the staffroom door. When it grinds open smile sweetly and inquire,

Note: there's no point in showing your teacher a pair of smelly sneakers. Ideally you should be holding a nice pair of shiny shoes for their inspection.

SHINY SHOES — YES!

SMELLY SNEAKERS — NO!

Answer:
Like any non-shiny object, leather is naturally bumpy and reflects light in all directions. That's why you can't see a clear reflection in it. The polish fills in the tiny dips in the leather to make a nice smooth surface that reflects light well and looks pretty spiffy.

Dare you discover . . . what a mirror does to light?

What you need:
A mirror
Two eyebrows and yourself

What you do:
1. Stand in front of the mirror.
2. Raise your left eyebrow. (If you can't do this just point to your left eyebrow instead.)

What does your reflection do?
a) It raises its left eyebrow.
b) The reflection raises its right eyebrow.
c) The reflection raises its right eyebrow but there's a delay of about half a second.

Answer:
b) That's because the light arriving from the right of a mirror always reflects to the left at the same angle. And, you got it — the light from the right leaves to the left. This means that you see the image in the mirror the wrong way around.

LIGHT ARRIVING FROM THE RIGHT REFLECTS TO THE LEFT →

LIGHT ARRIVING FROM THE LEFT REFLECTS TO THE RIGHT

This law of reflection was discovered long ago by a scientist born in what is now Iraq. Europeans call him Alhazen but his proper name was Abu al-Hassan ibn al-Haytham. Here's his story.

Hall of fame: Ibn al-Haytham (965-1040)
Nationality: Arab

Although he was a great scientist al-Haytham was
unlucky enough to serve a mad ruler — Egyptian Caliph
al-Hakim (985-1021).

According to an old story, one day the scientist
boasted to the Caliph that he could build a dam across the
River Nile. Big mistake. The Caliph sent al-Haytham to
southern Egypt but there he realized there was no
suitable site for the dam. There were too many waterfalls.
When al-Haytham returned to admit failure the Caliph
was furious. He made the scientist stand on a bench and
he had the bench hacked to pieces. The Caliph made it
horribly clear that al-Haytham was lucky not to be
hacked to pieces himself.

The Caliph gave al-Haytham an obscure government
job. But the Caliph was not a man to cross and the
scientist decided on a plan to save his life. He pretended
to go mad. Al-Haytham was locked up and the Caliph
forgot to have him killed. Ironically, a few years later the
Caliph went mad himself and was murdered by an
unknown hand. Afterwards al-Haytham told everyone
that he had just been pretending.

The boring truth?

Of course, some boring historians say this is just a story that people told after the scientist's death. Al-Haytham never mentioned it in any of his writings. But then why should he? He'd probably have wanted to forget the incident. And why should he risk raking up the past? What do you think?

The scientist got a job teaching at the Azhar mosque and copying ancient Greek manuscripts. And there he became interested in light. So he wrote a book called *The Treasury of Optics* in which he described his brilliant discoveries. (Unfortunately, he didn't describe his experiments in any detail.)

The Treasury of Optics
by Ibn al-Haytham

I'm not one to boast but I'm forced to admit that I am a brilliant scientist. I have found secrets about light that no one has ever discovered before. And what's more, I have proved all this by mathematical calculations and through experiments using mirrors that I made with my very own hands.

1. Light is given out by glowing objects. Some of the ancient Greek writers believed that light came from the eye and it was this that made the object glow. But I, Ibn al-Haytham have proved them all wrong!

2. Light travels in a straight line. Now as I said, I'm not one to blow my own trumpet - but this was one of my most ingenious and clever experiments. I made a hole in my wall so that the shaft of light entered the room. Then I checked the shaft of light and found it was perfectly straight. Brilliant!

3. Light always reflects at a predictable angle. By the most careful and painstaking measurements worthy only of the highest genius I have proved that if light shines from the left of a mirror it will bounce off to the right or vice-versa. And always at the same mathematically predictable angle.

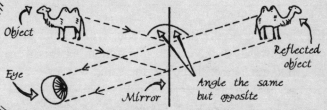

Object

Reflected object

Eye

Mirror

Angle the same but opposite

Although I'm really a very humble, modest person I am sure the name of Ibn al-Haytham will live for ever in history and all the world will want to read of my discoveries!

But people elsewhere in the world weren't interested in light and it took 200 years for al-Haytham's book to even appear in the West. Could you be a scientist like al-Haytham and discover the secrets of reflections? Here's your chance.

Dare you discover . . . how mirrors can change your appearance?

What you need:
A shiny tablespoon

What you do:
1. Hold the spoon like a hand mirror.
2. Look in the back of the spoon and then the front.

What do you notice?
a) My face appears upside-down in the back of the spoon and the right way up in the front.
b) My face appears fatter in the back of the spoon and upside-down with a long neck in the front of the spoon.
c) My face appears normal in the back of the spoon. In the front of the spoon I'm the right way up but I have a huge nose.

Answer:
b) The front of the spoon is concave — that is, it curves inwards at the center. (To remember this word just imagine a cave shaped in the same way.)

Because of this shape, light reflecting from your face reflects downwards from the top of the spoon and upwards from the bottom.

You see the bottom of your face at the top of the spoon and the top at the bottom. And your face appears upside-down. Turn the spoon around and you're faced with a bulging or as scientists say a convex shape.

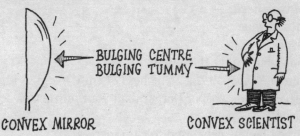

BULGING CENTRE
BULGING TUMMY

CONVEX MIRROR

CONVEX SCIENTIST

The convex shape reflects the light from your face and spreads it slightly outwards. This makes your face appear rounder and fatter (though this time you're the right way up!).

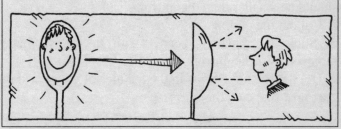

Dare you discover . . . how to make a ghost appear?

(This experiment is so good you'll want to do it again and again. All in the interest of science, of course.)

What you need:

Adhesive tape

Scissors

A small but bright flashlight

A mirror — about $9\frac{1}{2}$ x 14 inches (24 cm x 36 cm) is ideal.

A piece of black paper (larger than your mirror).

A pencil

A large black water-based felt-tip marker.

A room with light-colored walls.

What you do:

1. Draw the outline of your ghost on the black paper. This should be smaller than the mirror.

2. Cut out the outline.

3. Stick the remaining paper with the ghost shape removed over the mirror.

4. Use the felt tip to draw in the features of your ghost in the ghost shape on the mirror.

5. Darken the room. Better still wait until nightfall — after all, that's when ghosts appear.

IS NOW OK?   SURE!

6. Prop the mirror securely on an armchair. The mirror should be facing the wall about 6.5 feet (two meters) away. Shine your flashlight at the mirror. Your ghost appears on the wall.

7. Move the flashlight so the ghost appears to float in the air.

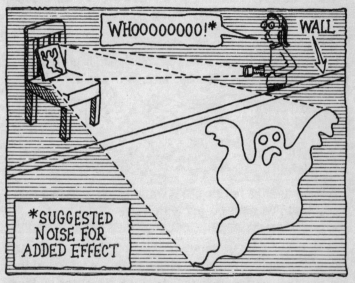

What is the scientific explanation for the ghost?

a) The flashlight light reflects off the black paper and the felt-tip lines.

b) The light reflects off the mirror but not the paper or the lines.

c) The light reflects off everything.

HORRIBLE HEALTH WARNING!

1. Don't try this experiment until you've checked with your parents it's OK to draw on the mirror. Defacing your granny's priceless antique mirror could prove fatal.

2. Be careful when handling the mirror. Mirrors are glass (surprise, surprise) and they can break and injure people. And give you seven years bad luck, so it's said.

DRAT! I HAVEN'T BROKEN A MIRROR FOR SIX YEARS, ELEVEN MONTHS AND THIRTY DAYS

WOW, THAT'S BAD LUCK, THEN!

3. Make sure the felt-tip pen is water based. It should be possible to wipe the ink off with water.

Since we're talking about frightening things, I should warn you about the next chapter. Beware — lurking among the weird facts in the chapter is a sinister-looking spider.

Will it frighten the socks off you? Read on and find out.

ARGH!

FRIGHTENING LIGHT-BENDERS

What do all these things have in common?

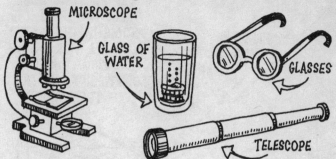

Yes, I know they all contain glass but that *isn't* the only CORRECT answer. Give up? Well, the other answer is that they all bend or refract light. But how do they do it?

Well, bend your eyes to this.

Frightening light fact file

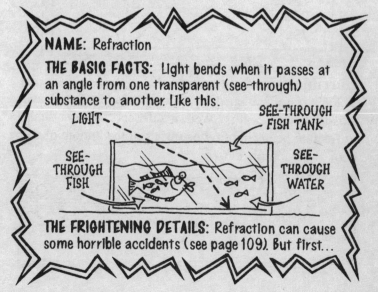

NAME: Refraction

THE BASIC FACTS: Light bends when it passes at an angle from one transparent (see-through) substance to another. Like this.

LIGHT

SEE-THROUGH FISH TANK

SEE-THROUGH FISH

SEE-THROUGH WATER

THE FRIGHTENING DETAILS: Refraction can cause some horrible accidents (see page 109). But first...

Here's a slow-motion replay of refraction as light hits that fish tank.

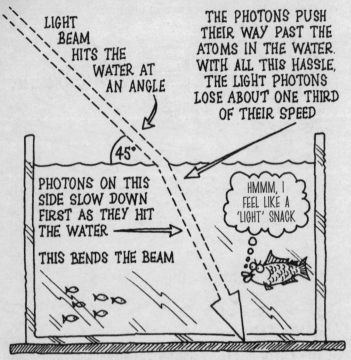

LIGHT BEAM HITS THE WATER AT AN ANGLE

THE PHOTONS PUSH THEIR WAY PAST THE ATOMS IN THE WATER. WITH ALL THIS HASSLE, THE LIGHT PHOTONS LOSE ABOUT ONE THIRD OF THEIR SPEED

45°

PHOTONS ON THIS SIDE SLOW DOWN FIRST AS THEY HIT THE WATER →

THIS BENDS THE BEAM

HMMM, I FEEL LIKE A 'LIGHT' SNACK

Horrible refraction accidents

1. Ever stare straight down into a swimming pool and wonder how deep it is? Well, it's deeper than you think. Refraction bends light reflecting from the bottom of the pool. So it appears closer.

I'M JUST GOING WADING, MOM. . .

2. Told you...

3. You can see this effect if you stare down at your legs in the water. They appear stumpy and short. It's true — honest, I'm not pulling your leg.

YIKES, THE COLD MUST HAVE MADE MY FEET SWELL UP!

4. In South America, and parts of the Pacific and Africa people fish with spears but thanks to refraction the fish often get away. And accidents do happen.

Refraction causes mirages. In hot places like deserts a layer of warm air forms over the ground. But above this the air can be much colder. Light from the sky speeds up and bends sideways as it passes from the cooler to the hotter air. As a result, light from the sky shines along the ground. And thirsty travelers see this light as a watery-looking blue on the horizon.

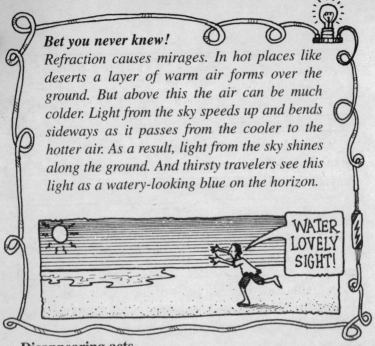

WATER LOVELY SIGHT!

Disappearing acts

But refraction can do even weirder things. Like making objects disappear. Oh, so you don't believe me, well, try this.

Dare you discover ... how to make a coin disappear?

What you need:

A coin

A sink

A ruler

OK, AS LONG AS IT DOESN'T DISAPPEAR AT THE CANDY STORE

What you do:

1. Fill the sink with water to a depth of 1.6 inches (4 cm).

2. Place the coin in the water.

3. Crouch down so that you can just barely see the coin over the rim of the sink.

4. Lift the plug slightly so the water level in the sink falls slowly.

As the water goes down the drain the coin gradually disappears. *Why?*

a) Grrrr! My coin has gone down the drain!

b) The water refracted the light reflecting back from the coin so it made the coin look further away than it really was.

c) The light from the coin was refracted so the coin appeared closer.

Answer:
c) The water bent the light toward you so the coin appeared closer. As the water drained away the light refracted less. The coin appeared to move away until it disappeared behind the rim. But actually the coin didn't move.

If refraction can make coins vanish then maybe it can make a larger object disappear. Perhaps even a human being? Here's a story in which this happens — but is it true? What do you think?

Now you see me, now you don't

LONDON, 1897

Tonight I became invisible. As I watched my own body disappear I remembered how hard I worked under cover of darkness so no one could steal my ideas. All those years of frustration and poverty and disappointment. Now, at last I have succeeded.

It was a strange, frightening experience.

First I took drugs for several days to remove all the color pigments from my body. My skin and hair turned snow white. (Even now the side-effects cause me pain.) Then I stood between two electrical power sources. These make the strange invisible rays that I have discovered. Rays that alter the atoms of water in my body so they no longer refract light. In this way, light shines straight through my body as if I were made of air.

As the rays fell on my body I felt I was becoming a ghost. My white face and hair slowly grew dimmer until I could see nothing in the mirror. The skin of my arms and legs looked like glass – I could see the fat and nerves beneath.

And gradually everything faded away until I could stand before the mirror and see nothing but an empty room. . .

Answer:
Great story, isn't it? It's based on *The Invisible Man* by H.G. Wells (1866-1946). But it's only a story because: **1.** The rays described don't exist. **2.** If the scientist had no pigments then he wouldn't have pigments in his retina to help him see. **3.** The lens and cornea of the eye refract light and focus it on to the retina. (Remember that bit from page 45?) But if the scientist's invisible body didn't refract light then these parts of his eye wouldn't refract it either. So he couldn't see the room.

Brilliant lenses

Assuming you're not invisible, lenses are a great way to refract light. They come in two main varieties, convex and concave. (Remember these words?)

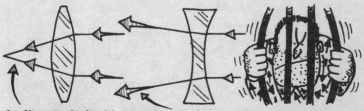

CONVEX LENS LIGHT BENDS INWARDS

CONCAVE LENS LIGHT BENDS OUTWARDS

CONVICT LEN BENDS BARS

OK, let's take a peek through these lenses. And here's a particularly revolting hairy spider to study.

1. Through a convex lens the spider appears bigger. Let's take a look at the spider's head.

2. Light reflects off the spider's ugly little mug.

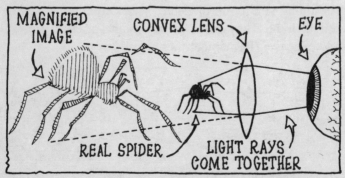

The convex lens bends this light towards a single point.

3. If you put your eye at this point you'll see a close-up view of the spider's head with eight huge beady eyes staring back at you. YIKES!

Let's use a concave lens to take another look at the spider. Yes, it's all in the interest of Science.

1. This lens spreads the light wider.

2. And when you look through the lens the spider appears much smaller. Phew! Not so bad — ?

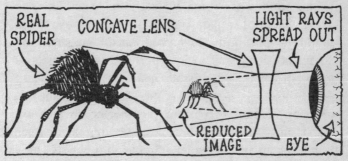

So concave lenses make things look smaller and convex lenses make them look bigger. And not surprisingly you find convex lenses in cameras, binoculars, telescopes, microscopes and tons of scientific instruments which make things appear larger.

Of course, if you're wearing glasses to read this page you'll know all about lenses. You've got two of them perched on the end of your nose. But why wear them?

Frightening expressions

An ophthalmologist says,

YOU MAY HAVE HYPEROPIA, MYOPIA OR ASTIGMATISM

Are any of these fatal?

Answer:

No, they're eye problems caused by faulty focusing.

1. Hyperopia means that you're far-sighted. The lens of your eye doesn't bend light enough. This means that it can't focus light from close objects onto your retina. So close up objects look blurred. A similar effect can be caused if your eyeball is too short.

2. Myopia is near-sightedness. That's when the light reflecting from a distant object gets bent too far by your lens and distant objects seem blurred. A similar effect can be caused if your eyeball is too long.

3. Astigmatism is when the cornea is slightly out of shape. This results in part of the image appearing blurred.

If you have any of these you'll need to wear glasses or contact lenses to correct the problem. Cheer up you'll look very brainy and they're scientifically fascinating.

Spectacular spectacles

1. The first glasses to be invented had convex lenses. They were probably invented in Italy in the thirteenth century and worn by far-sighted people.

2. As you've just discovered, the far-sighted eye has a lens that doesn't bend the light inward enough to focus an image on the retina.

A convex lens bends the light further inward to focus an image.

3. Concave lenses were first made in around 1451. German churchman Nicholas of Cusa (1401-1464) worked out that this shape could help near-sighted people. What a far-sighted man!

4. A near-sighted eye lens pushes the light inward too much. So the light focuses before it gets to the retina.

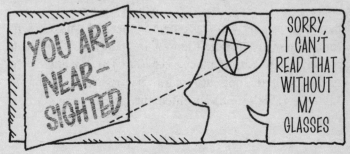

The concave lens spreads the light so it focuses on the retina.

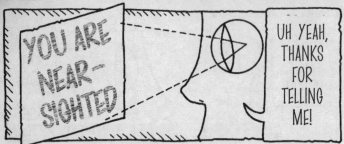

5. Contact lenses do the same job as glasses. Nowadays they're slices of soft watery plastic that fit over the eyeball. But the first lenses invented by German Adolf Fick (1829-1901) in 1888 were made of glass. The glass rubbed against the eyeballs and made them sore. What a sight for sore eyes!

6. And Adolf even managed to make lenses of exactly the right shape to fit over the eyeball and bend light on to the retina. The answer was to shape the lenses in moulds made by using the eyeballs of dead people.

7. DON'T WORRY! Your local optician DOESN'T have a drawer full of eyeballs. Nowadays, they measure the curve of your eyeballs using a keratometer. This instrument directs a beam of light into your eyeball (which reflects it) and records the position of the reflected light. This data is used to calculate its exact curve.

8. Not surprisingly, it was a pair of spectacle makers who found a new use for their lenses. In 1608 Dutch spectacle maker, Hans Lippershey (1570-1618) invented the telescope and soon afterward his assistant Zacharius Jannsen (1580-1638) invented the microscope. Or did they?

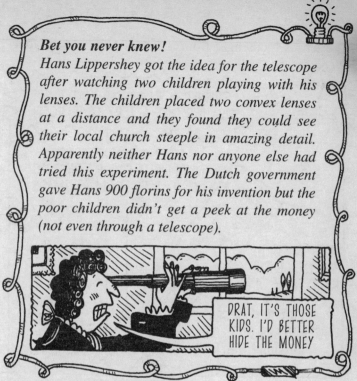

Anyway, speaking of telescopes...

Frightening expressions

Sounds frightening. Could this mean the end of the world? No. Chromatic aberration means he's got a problem with his telescope. It's caused by different-size light waves being refracted by different amounts.

A traditional telescope has two or more convex lenses.

The lenses focus light from a distant object on to your eyeball.

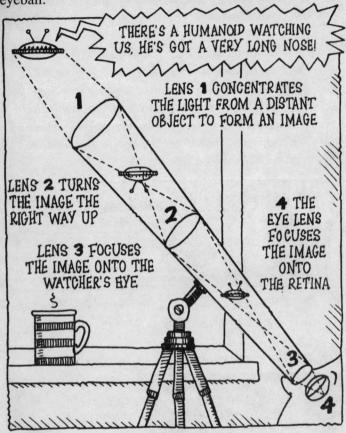

But here's the problem. Because different colored lights refract at different angles, they don't all focus in exactly the same spot. So images would have a colored "halo" around the edge — and that's chromatic aberration.

Luckily for astronomers, Isaac Newton solved this problem in 1668. He designed a telescope that used a concave mirror to focus the light instead of a lens.

Because mirrors reflect all wavelengths in the same way, there was no "halo" around the image. And Newton's design is still in use today.

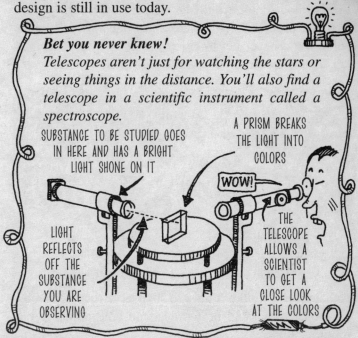

Bet you never knew!
Telescopes aren't just for watching the stars or seeing things in the distance. You'll also find a telescope in a scientific instrument called a spectroscope.

SUBSTANCE TO BE STUDIED GOES IN HERE AND HAS A BRIGHT LIGHT SHONE ON IT

A PRISM BREAKS THE LIGHT INTO COLORS

WOW!

LIGHT REFLECTS OFF THE SUBSTANCE YOU ARE OBSERVING

THE TELESCOPE ALLOWS A SCIENTIST TO GET A CLOSE LOOK AT THE COLORS

Talking of colors you'd better read the next chapter. It's full of crucial colorful facts. Yep, color is CRUCIAL — I mean, where would drivers be if they couldn't tell the difference between a green and a red light? In the hospital that's where!

Well, you've got the green light to turn the page.

READY GET SET TURN!

CRUCIAL COLOURS

Life without color would be frighteningly boring. Just like an endless awful, old black and white movie. Without color you'd never get to enjoy the glory of a peacock's tail, a glowing sunset, or a garden full of flowers.

Although you wouldn't have to shudder at the frightening crimson, purple, and brown decor in your aunt's living room.

A NOTE TO THE READER

We apologize for the loss of color. Readers will have to imagine the wonderful glowing, vibrant colors described in these pages. And if you do get bored you can always color them in.
P.S. If it's not your book go and buy your own before you pick up your crayons. Anyway, here's how light makes color appear.

Frightening light fact file

NAME: Colors

THE BASIC FACTS: 1. White light contains all the colors in the rainbow — remember that bit? In fact, each color is caused by a light wave of a particular size.

2. When light hits an object some of the colors are soaked up and others are reflected. And it's the reflected colors that we see. Got all that?

THE FRIGHTENING DETAILS: When something is black all the colors in light are soaked up so nothing reflects back. This explains the color of this big black revolting slug.

YEAH, CHEERS!

Read on for more colorful facts.

The colorful facts

A green leaf or caterpillar soaks up all the colors in light except green. Green reflects off the leaf (or caterpillar) and that's what you see.

GREEN PLANT

GARDENER'S GREEN FINGERS

GREEN CATERPILLAR

White objects reflect every kind of light. (Don't forget white light is all the colors mixed up.)

POLAR BEAR IN THE SNOW (WEARING A WHITE BOBBLE HAT).

Bet you never knew!
1. Windows, plastic bags, and bottles don't reflect colors. They're see-through, or "transparent," as a scientist would say. With a see-through material, such as glass, the atoms form thin layers or are regularly spaced so most light gets through. That's how light manages to shine through your window — it's transparently obvious.
2. Some fish are transparent. For example, the X-ray fish, found in South American rivers, has no pigments. This allows it to hide from attackers. The fish is a bit like the Invisible Man on page 112 except you can see its skeleton and guts through the skin.

I ADMIRE YOUR GUTS

YOURS LOOK PRETTY COOL, TOO!

Dare you discover . . . where color comes from?

What you need:

A nice juicy red tomato

A piece of white paper

A small but bright flashlight

What you do:

1. Darken the room or better still wait for nightfall.

2. Place the tomato on one end of the paper.

3. Hold the flashlight over the paper level with the tomato. Shine the light on the tomato.

4. Look at the area of shadow under the flashlight beam. It should be glowing pink. *Why?*

a) The tomato is reflecting red light on to the paper.

b) It's a trick of my eyes caused by the flashlight light.

c) The shadow of the tomato is soaking up all the colors in light except red.

Answer: **a)** White paper reflects all the colors of light that fall on it. The pink glow is due to the red light reflecting off the tomato and onto the paper. All the other colors in the light get soaked up by the tomato. The experiment proves that colors are indeed caused by the reflection of light.

Most objects, though, reflect a mix of different colored light. Take bananas, for example.

Teacher's lunchtime teaser

You will need a banana and a lot of courage. Knock loudly on the staffroom door. When it squeaks open put on your most innocent expression and ask,

Answer:
Well, it might appear yellow but it actually reflects red and green light and soaks up blue light. Your eyes see this mix of red and green as yellow. (You can find out how on pages 134-135.)

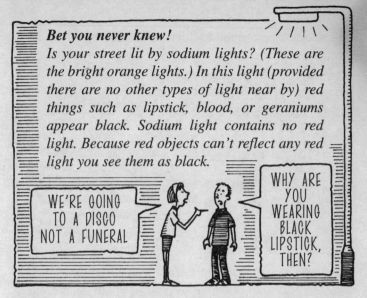

Bet you never knew!

Is your street lit by sodium lights? (These are the bright orange lights.) In this light (provided there are no other types of light near by) red things such as lipstick, blood, or geraniums appear black. Sodium light contains no red light. Because red objects can't reflect any red light you see them as black.

WE'RE GOING TO A DISCO NOT A FUNERAL

WHY ARE YOU WEARING BLACK LIPSTICK, THEN?

Talking about reflecting colors, did you know two scientists spent their vacation reflecting on this very topic? That's sad.

Hall of fame: Chandrasekhara Vankata Raman (1888-1970) Nationality: Indian
John Strutt, Lord Rayleigh (1824-1919)
Nationality: British

You couldn't find two more different characters than C.V. Raman and John Strutt.

Raman was a brilliant scientist but he had to work for the Indian civil service as a young man because of a shortage of scientific jobs in India. (In 1917 he became Professor of Physics at Calcutta University.) Strutt was a rich lord with a private laboratory in his mansion and a top university job in England. They worked separately to solve two tricky light questions but by an odd coincidence Raman later became friendly with Strutt's son.

The questions sound childishly simple.

But these questions aren't stupid and the answers are frighteningly complicated, as you're about to discover. In 1871 John Strutt went on vacation to Egypt. Cruising through the Mediterranean, he admired the lovely blue sky and sea.

Being a scientist, though, he did more than enjoy what he saw. He used his scientific know-how to explain it. His letter home might have read like this:

To Lord & Lady Rayleigh,
Tering Place, Essex, England.

Dear Mom and Dad,
Having a great vacation! I've read lots
of science books and there's plenty
of interesting sights to fascinate a
budding scientist like me. Like the
blue sky and sea, for example. I
mean, what makes them so blue? I
suspect atoms in the air reflect
light. I think blue light is
scattered much better than other
lights (I'm not sure why) so we see
more of it. I think the sea is blue
because it reflects the sky.
    Oh, I forgot to say, the cruise is OK.
Yours scientifically,
John

Notes to the reader...

1. John was right. Blue light photons have more energy
and this makes them more likely to bounce off the atoms
downwards and into our eyes. So we get to see more blue
light photons when we look at the sky. And that makes
the sky appear blue. Honest, it's a true-blue fact!.

2. But sunsets aren't blue — are they? Well, this actually
proves John Strutt was right. When the sun is low we see
its light shining at an angle through all the old dust in the
air. The dust reflects away most of the blue photons

before the light gets to us. But who cares? We get to enjoy the reddish-orange colors that were in the sunlight and didn't get reflected upward so much.

OK, now back to the story.

In 1921, Raman was sailing to a science conference in Britain. Feeling rather bored he decided to test John Strutt's findings about the sea. By this time the older scientist was dead so Raman couldn't drop him a postcard. But he might have written to his pal John Strutt's scientist son, Robert Strutt, the next Lord Rayleigh (1875-1947).

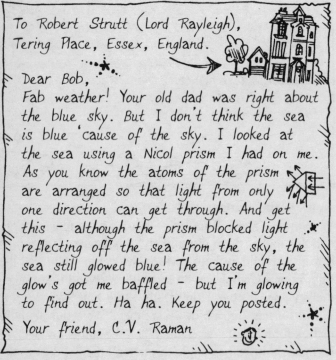

To Robert Strutt (Lord Rayleigh),
Tering Place, Essex, England.

Dear Bob,
Fab weather! Your old dad was right about the blue sky. But I don't think the sea is blue 'cause of the sky. I looked at the sea using a Nicol prism I had on me. As you know the atoms of the prism are arranged so that light from only one direction can get through. And get this — although the prism blocked light reflecting off the sea from the sky, the sea still glowed blue! The cause of the glow's got me baffled — but I'm glowing to find out. Ha ha. Keep you posted.
Your friend, C.V. Raman

So why *was* the sea blue?

Back at his lab in 1922 Raman did a series of experiments that involved shining light through water and found the answer.

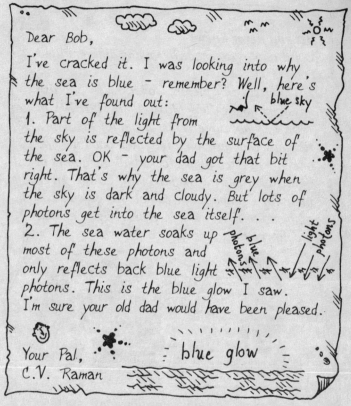

Dear Bob,

I've cracked it. I was looking into why the sea is blue – remember? Well, here's what I've found out:

1. Part of the light from the sky is reflected by the surface of the sea. OK – your dad got that bit right. That's why the sea is grey when the sky is dark and cloudy. But lots of photons get into the sea itself. . .

2. The sea water soaks up most of these photons and only reflects back blue light photons. This is the blue glow I saw.

I'm sure your old dad would have been pleased.

Your Pal,
C.V. Raman

For Raman, it must have seemed that the sky (and the sea) was the limit. He went on to find how bonds between atoms in a chemical can affect an atom's wobble and add or remove energy from the reflecting photons. And in 1930 he won the Nobel Prize for this work.

Mysterious color mixing

On their own, colors are fairly straightforward. But try mixing them together and the facts get murky.

Bet you never knew!
Color photos are made by mixing different light colors.
1. The first color picture was taken by Scottish physicist James Clerk Maxwell (1831-1879). In 1863 he took three shots of one of his wife's ribbons. One through a red filter, one blue and one green. Each filter blocked all the colors in light except its particular color. So the green filter, for example, showed only the green parts of the pattern. He combined the images to make a color picture.

FASCINATING, CAN I HAVE IT BACK NOW?

2. Nowadays, though, color film consist of three layers of chemicals. The top layer makes a blue color from blue light, the second makes green in the same way, and the third makes a red color. Between them the chemicals build up an image. Our brains do the rest of the color mixing — as you'll discover on pages 134-135.

Muddy mixed-up paints

But just imagine that you tried to make a painting in the same way as a photo. You carefully mixed thin layers of blue, green, and red. And produced a muddy black smear.

Want to know why? Why not ask your art teacher.

Test your art teacher

If you mix green and red and blue light together you'll get a pale whitish sort of a color. But if you mix together green and red and blue paints you get black — why?

Answer:
White light is made up of all colors. So the more colors of light you mix the closer you get to white light. But paints and other colored objects (like tomatoes and bananas) work by soaking up some light colors and reflecting others. So the more paints you add to your mix the closer you get to something that soaks up every color in light. In other words — black.

Crucial color vision

Whatever colors you manage to mix you'll need a pair of eyes to appreciate them. Humans, birds and apes are lucky in this respect. We view the world in glorious living Technicolor. Unlike for example, a squid, which can only see black and white or your pet cat who sees green and blue but not red. (Scientists aren't quite sure why this is — but when Twinkie finishes off a mouse she sees the blood and gory bits as green.)

How you see in color

1. Unlike Twinkie you've actually got three types of cone cells in your retina — one each for green, blue and red light. All the colors you see are made from mixing at least two of these colors. (For more info. on mixing light see page 126.)

2. Your incredible eyes are able to make out up to ten million different colors. It's amazing to think they can do this from just three basic colors. Here's your chance to test this remarkable ability.

Dare you discover . . . how you see colors?

What you need:

A piece of black paper

A small piece of yellow paper about 1.2 inches (3 cm) square.

Your head complete with eyeballs.

What you do:

1. Place the yellow paper on the black paper and stare at it for 30 seconds without moving your head or blinking.
2. You should see a square of blue appearing around the edge of the yellow square.

OK, so where does it come from?
a) The cells that fire blue signals take time to work — but now they've detected blue coloring in the black paper.
b) The yellow paper has excited your blue cells so much they've gone into overdrive. And now you're seeing too much blue.
c) The green and red cells that give you yellow are getting tired but the blue cells are still firing.

Answer:
c) Your eye sees yellow by firing green and red cone cells (remember the banana?). Your brain mixes these sensations to make yellow. But after a while the cells become less sensitive. Meanwhile blue cone cells are still firing in this area of your retina so you see a blue image. You see "after-images" for the same reason. Mind you — it took a few disgusting eyeball experiments before scientists worked this out.

Eyeball to eyeball
WARNING: DISGUSTING FACTS COMING UP. (Hopefully your breakfast won't be coming up after you read them.)
Isaac Newton believed we see colors by changing the shape of our eyeballs. Isaac thought this helped the eye to refract white light into colored light that then fell on the retina.

To test this idea Isaac stuck what might have been a toothpick under his eyeball. A toothpick is a stick for getting bits of food out from between your teeth. Isaac's toothpick was probably encrusted with millions of germs and the stale remains of his dinner. YUCK!

Using the toothpick Isaac squeezed his own eyeball to change its shape. He saw a few lights, but not enough to prove his theory.

The germs on the toothpick infected his eyeball. It became so painful that he had to go to bed for two weeks. This proves that even a scientific genius can do very stupid things.

More colorful scientists

After Newton, other famous scientists probed color
vision. The story continues with British chemist John
Dalton (1766-1844). John Dalton was one of the first
people to suggest that there were such things as atoms.
But come to think of it, he wasn't too colorful himself.

A fellow scientist said:

HIS STYLE OF
WRITING AND
CONVERSATION
ARE DRY

Nowadays we might call him "boring." Boring John
loved to study flowers. Unfortunately, he found that he
couldn't see red colors properly.

IT'S
BLUE

IT'S
RED

NO NEED
TO GET
ALL BLUE
IN THE
FACE
ABOUT IT

John suffered from color blindness — a condition that
affects about one in 25 people and he enjoyed giving
boring lectures on the subject. According to John color
blindness was caused by a build-up of blue juice in the
eyeball. The blue color soaks up red light.

He made arrangements for his eyeballs to be removed after his death to check for blue juice.

Meanwhile our old pal Thomas Young had been treating patients with color blindness. As a result of this work he believed the retina had separate regions that detected red, blue and violet. And Dalton had a problem with his red region.

Unfortunately Young died before Dalton's eyeballs were removed so he never knew the result. In fact, the jelly in Dalton's eyeballs proved to be nice and clear. Dalton would have been dead disappointed if he wasn't already dead.

The mystery solved

The mystery was solved by another famous scientist, James Clerk Maxwell. He spun a disc divided into green and red and blue sections. The colors appeared to merge into white. People who couldn't see the color red saw white in a spinning disc that had only blue and green sections. This proved:

1. That the cone cells in our eyes can see green, blue and red light.

2. That they make all the other colors from these three. (The white color was a mix of all the other colors.)

3. In color-blind people one type of cone cell is missing or not working properly.

Bet you never knew!
As long as your vision's working OK you're bound to enjoy a multi-colored laser show. By using different chemicals in lasers scientists can change the color of this light. For example, atoms of ruby produce red light. But you can't enjoy the pretty colors by gazing directly into a laser beam. It's so bright it would probably blind you or heat up your eyeball until it boils.

Dare you take a closer look at lasers? Why not turn to the next frightening chapter?

ER, OK THEN...

As you're about to find out, lasers are a huge part of modern life and they're ready to brighten up our future too. Like all great inventions, lasers began with a flash of inspiration.

A laser flash of inspiration

In 1951 U.S. scientist Charles H. Townes was at a scientific conference in Washington.

I'M TRYING TO PRODUCE HIGH-POWERED RADIO WAVES THAT CAN BE USED TO STUDY THE STRUCTURE OF ATOMS

FASCINATING!

That night Townes couldn't sleep. His mind was working overtime on the problem. So very early the next morning before it got light he went for a walk and ended up on a park bench. He was looking for inspiration.

THINK! THINK!

Suddenly he found it. Townes scribbled his ideas on the back of an old envelope. If you could control the speed the atoms wobble and keep the light from escaping you could create a powerful beam of light. Since radio waves are made by photons you could do the same things with radio waves.

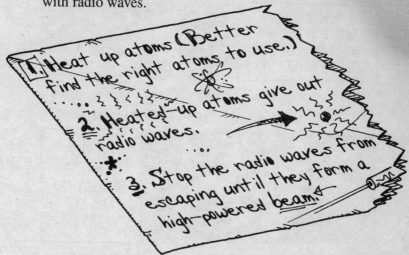

Townes later found out he had been sitting opposite of the house of famous inventor Alexander Graham Bell (1847-1922). And Townes wondered if the dead inventor had provided ghostly assistance.

Later Townes realized that you could use light instead of radio waves. By 1958, working with his brother-in-law, Arthur Schawlow, Townes had worked out how a laser might work. He even coined the name "laser" over lunch. But he had little idea of how useful the laser would become. He later said:

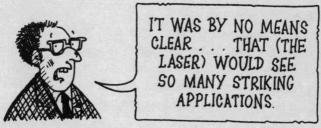

For scientists at the time, building a laser just seemed to be a fascinating technical challenge.

In 1960 another U.S. physicist, Theodore Maiman, used Townes's plans to build the world's first working laser.

In 1964 Townes won the Nobel Prize for his work together with two Russian scientists, Nikolai Basov and Alexander Prokhorov who developed the laser separately but at the same time.

Interesting postscript:
Actually, unknown to Townes, the idea of a laser and perhaps even the name had been dreamt up by another U.S. scientist, Gordon Gould in 1957. Unfortunately, Gould didn't publish his idea and he didn't take out a patent in time so he missed out on the glory.

Laser defense systems

Lasers have lots of uses. One purpose developed by the military is a laser defense system to shoot down enemy missiles. Sounds exciting? Well, here's how to defend your school from hostile attack with a laser defense system.

HORRIBLE HEALTH WARNINGS!

1. Laser beams can sizzle human flesh. Do not direct your laser beam anywhere near a teacher or any other poor defenseless creatures.

2. This laser is highly destructive. You can only read this section if you promise to use your laser system to PROTECT your school. And NOT to vaporize the buildings before science class on Monday.

How to make your own laser defense system

TOP SECRET INSTRUCTIONS – KEEP OUT OF REACH OF TEACHERS

Step 1 — assemble your materials.

To build your own laser defense system you will need:

A power supply

A box lined with mirrors. Leave a partly-silvered mirror in one end for your laser to shine through.

Something to produce light photons (a block of ruby will do).

A bucket of water.

You will also need:

A high-speed jet plane complete with pilot and a

computer controlled high sensitivity heat detecting system. (You may be able to borrow these from your local air force base.)

Step 2 — assemble your laser.
1. Place the ruby in the box and link it up to your power supply.

2. OK, this is the part that you've been waiting for. Flick the switch and turn on your power supply.
3. The power surge makes the atoms in the ruby wobble violently. They give out photons of red light. These bump into more atoms which wobble and make more photons.
4. A growing crowd of photons charges up and down the inside of the box reflecting off the mirrors. Eventually the light is so bright the photons actually flash *through* the mirror as a blinding beam of light.
5. All this power makes your ruby very hot. If your machine shows signs of over-heating simply dump the water on it. (Some lasers have built-in water cooling systems.)

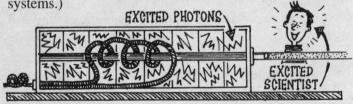

Step 3 — how to shoot down missiles.

1. Simply get your plane in the air and keep an eye out for incoming missiles. You can use your heat detecting system to track the heat blasting from behind the enemy missile.

2. When you spot a missile aim the laser at its fuel tank. Try to keep the beam steady for a few seconds. The laser's heat will melt the missile's side and set fire to its fuel. The enemy missile will then blow up in mid-air and you'll have saved your school.

EXCELLENT JENKINS. I'LL MAKE SURE YOU GET A GOOD REPORT THIS TERM.

Making light work

Of course, your laser can do much more than zap enemy missiles. In fact, lasers can make light work of many jobs.

1. A laser beam makes a snappy-snipper! Lasers are used in factories to cut fabric at 49 feet (15 m) a second.

2. Laser beams read bar codes in stores or libraries. Take a look on the back of this book. Can you see a square with a pattern of lines? The pattern is a unique code for *Frightening Light*. If you bought the book you may have seen the shop assistant passing a scanner across the lines. A laser beam in the scanner flickers as it picks up the lines and the flickering beam is read by a computer that recognizes the code from the pattern of flickers. Here's an idea that's really on the right lines.

3. Lasers can be life-savers. They can cut through human flesh and heat seal the edges of a wound so you don't get bleeding. By firing a laser down an endoscope (that's a tube containing optical fibers, remember) you can perform life-saving operations deep within the body. A laser can even weld back a retina that has come adrift from the inside of the eyeball.

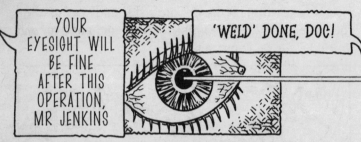

4. A laser beam "reads" a CD by flickering as it reflects off a pattern of pits on its surface. The CD player turns this flickering light signal into electric pulses and then into your favorite rock music.

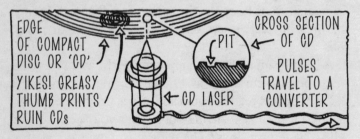

5. Laser beams travel in straight lines so you can use them to build nice straight tunnels. Simply fire a beam from the entrance of the tunnel and get digging along the line of the beam.

6. A laser beam can melt and weld metals. And unlike any other tool a laser beam never gets blunt with use.

7. Laser beams liven up rock concerts. Simply fire the laser into the air and wave it around to make dramatic light patterns. And then who cares if the music's terrible?

8. Lasers can measure tiny earthquakes. Lasers on the San Andreas Fault in California are linked up to monitoring equipment. Any wobble in the light beam caused by a tremor in the ground can be instantly detected.

9. Laser printers work by firing an image of the page you're printing on to a light-sensitive drum. This drum has an electrical force which then picks up toner (the black stuff) and prints onto the paper. And laser printers are fast — maybe that's because they keep in toner — ha ha.

But that's just the start of what lasers can do. They're so useful that scientists have really taken a shine to them, ha, ha.

Bet you never knew!

You can make holograms with lasers. All you have to do is...

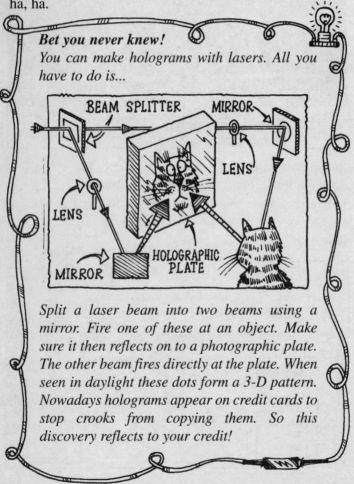

BEAM SPLITTER MIRROR

MIRROR

LENS

LENS

HOLOGRAPHIC PLATE

Split a laser beam into two beams using a mirror. Fire one of these at an object. Make sure it then reflects on to a photographic plate. The other beam fires directly at the plate. When seen in daylight these dots form a 3-D pattern. Nowadays holograms appear on credit cards to stop crooks from copying them. So this discovery reflects to your credit!

Speedy signals

Don't forget light is *FAST* with a capital F. And so is laser light.

• In 0.14 seconds you can send a laser signal around the world.

• In 2.5 seconds you can send a light signal to the moon *and* back again. (In the 1960s scientists did this. By timing the signal they were able to calculate the exact distance of the moon.)

• A laser could send a light signal to Mars in just three minutes. (The Martians' reply would take another three minutes.)

But laser signals aren't just for chatting with aliens. You probably use them to talk to your friends. Yes — every time you pick up a phone.

Listening lasers

When you talk into a phone connected to an optical fiber cable the same technology that turns a laser light into sound in a CD works in reverse.

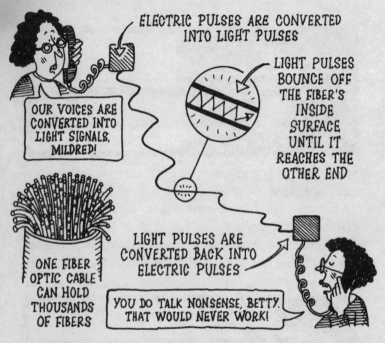

A microphone turns the sound of your voice into electric pulses which are transformed into laser light signals. These whiz down the cable.

At the other end of the line the process is reversed and you hear sounds in your ear.

And because light moves so fast and a laser can flicker at billions of times a second an optical fiber can carry a conversation down the line in the blink of an eye. And what's more, you can squash thousands of fibers into a single cable.

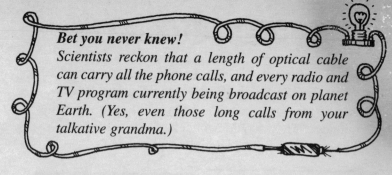

And yet the wonders of optical fibers look pale compared with future developments. But is the future bright with promise or is it dark and frightening? Let's gaze into the crystal ball.

A BRIGHTER FUTURE?

Imagine there was no light on planet Earth except for your pocket flashlight. People would grope their way through the darkness to marvel at this amazing brightness. They would wonder at its beauty and its ability to turn darkness into colors and shadows.

WE PRAISE YOU MISTRESS OF THE LIGHT. YOU SHINE YOUR WONDROUS BEAM ON OUR HUMBLE FACES

But light is everywhere. And because we see it every day we don't think too much about it. What a pity.

Light is awesome, unbelievable, fantastic. And although the science of light seems frightening at first — the more you discover the more magical it seems. It's incredible that a humble light bulb makes photons and that these astonishing blips of energy can light up the sky in the day and at night you can see stars because their photons have traveled for millions of years to reach you.

It's even more astonishing to think that it's photons that give color to a daffodil or power to a laser. And it's amazing to peer in a mirror and know that you can only see yourself because every second billions of photons are bouncing off the mirror to create an image made of light.

But the latest discoveries of physicists are even MORE exciting, even more brain-boggling. And they're about to light up our future in totally unexpected ways. For example:

1. Small is beautiful
Nowadays people can make a fiber-optic cable thousands of times finer than the eye of a needle. And tiny lasers are possible too. In 1989 IBM made a laser one-tenth the thickness of a human hair. With a bit of careful packing you could fit a *million* of them into this box.

The laser was made from tiny crystals and this technology will make possible micro-holograms and tiny surgical instruments for delicate operations. In fact, miniature versions of any machine that uses a laser.

2. Creative chemical chaos
U.S. and German scientists are learning to use lasers to trigger chemical reactions. Traditionally, you had to heat

things up over an old Bunsen burner like the sort you find in schools.

But by using laser pulses of exactly the right length scientists can break chemicals into smaller groups of atoms to create brand new chemicals. And this could turn every industry that uses chemical reactions upside down.

3. Marvels in store

Scientists are learning how to store light. As you know, light is always on the move. But in 1998 scientists at the University of Amsterdam trapped infrared light inside ground up crystals. Normally, atoms soak up or reflect light. But the ground up crystals form a maze of tiny spaces. The light photons chase in circles like captured beasts but they can't escape from the maze. That's a-mazing, isn't it?

4. The ultimate dream machine

This breakthrough could lead to the ultimate computer. A computer that calculates billions of sums at the speed of light using photons to send information. And scientists are already dreaming of such a machine. A machine millions of times more powerful than the fastest traditional computer. Just think, with a computer like that you could do your math homework in one second. That's progress for you!

Sure, light is the fastest moving thing in the universe. But science is beginning to catch up. The future's looking horribly bright — and that's the brilliant truth!